THE QUESTION

HENRI ALLEG

Translated from the French by
JOHN CALDER

Preface by
JEAN-PAUL SARTRE

With a new afterword by the author

FOREWORD TO THE BISON BOOKS EDITION BY
Ellen Ray

INTRODUCTION TO THE BISON BOOKS EDITION BY
James D. Le Sueur

UNIVERSITY OF NEBRASKA PRESS
LINCOLN AND LONDON

Published by arrangement with the Institute for Media Analysis, Inc.,
New York, under license from the Calder Educational Trust, Ltd.,
London.
© Editions de Minuit, 1958

© 1958 by John Calder [Publishers] Ltd.
Foreword, introduction, and afterword © 2006 by the Board of
Regents of the University of Nebraska
Manufactured in the United States of America

∞

First Nebraska paperback printing: 2006

Library of Congress Cataloging-in-Publication Data
Alleg, Henri.
[Question. English]
The question / Henri Alleg; translated from the French by John
Calder; preface by Jean-Paul Sartre.
p. cm.
Originally published London: John Calder Publishers Ltd., 1958.
ISBN-13: 978-0-8032-5960-7 (pbk.: alk. paper)
ISBN-10: 0-8032-5960-3 (pbk.: alk. paper)
1. Alleg, Henri. 2. Algeria—History—Revolution, 1954–1962—
Personal narratives, French. 3. Political prisoners—Algeria—
Biography. 4. Torture—Algeria—History—20th century. I. Title.
DT295.3.A537A313 2006
965'.0467—dc22 2005030220

This Bison Books edition follows the original in beginning chapter 1
on arabic page 33; the text remains unaltered.

CONTENTS

FOREWORD

Ellen Ray

Why republish, indeed, why read a book about a journalist who was tortured by French soldiers during the Algerian revolution of the 1950s? Henri Alleg's straightforward, unsentimental report of his experience when military authorities accused him of contacts with the Algerian national liberation movement is a classic of anticolonial literature. And as it happens, this book has something to say about our own postcolonial period as well.

Condemned by international law and in the rhetoric of the democratic, "civilized" West, torture is increasingly part of the arsenal of our military services. In fact, official Pentagon reports, originally classified, suggest that kidnappings, unlawful interrogations and punishments, and sometimes summary executions of prisoners are becoming routine practices by our security services, in and out of uniform, in George W. Bush's endless "war against terror."

The top military lawyers of the U.S. Army, Air Force, and Marine Corps have written scathing objections to the Defense and Justice Departments' definition of torture and of acceptable interrogation techniques, and the State Department expressed concern that the Geneva Conventions were being abrogated.

Subsequent news reports about heinous abuses in the U.S. military prisons at Abu Ghraib in Iraq, Baghram in Afghanistan, and Guantanamo in Cuba rightly scandalized the American public. And there is mounting evidence that this behavior is just the tip of an iceberg that our national security establishment has been forced to reveal. So far, some light punishment has been meted out to a few hapless soldiers, scarcely responsible for the larger strategy, a strategy that incorporates racism, torture, and murder in a war that is increasingly fought as a "them-or-us" struggle. As such, it reduces the human worth of "them" while equating questioning of "us" with a lack of patriotism, or even treason.

Some of the military's own defense attorneys, as well as some FBI agents, have charged that prisoners are chained to the floor for days on end, deprived of food and drink, subjected to endless noise and light. They are denied medical attention if they refuse to cooperate with their interrogators. They are manipulated, humiliated, sexually taunted and shamed, and their religion defiled. They are subjected to what a Pentagon investigation called "sadistic, blatant, and wanton" abuses, including attacks by dogs, rape, sodomy, and, sometimes, death. Frequently, prisoners are subjected to "rendition"—being sent clandestinely to other countries to be tortured by foreign interrogators on our behalf.

The 1984 United Nations Convention Against Torture, ratified by the United States in 1994, defines torture as "any act by which severe pain or suffering, whether physical or mental, is intentionally inflicted on a person for such purposes as obtaining from him or a third person information or a confession, punishing him for an act he or a third person has committed or is suspected of having committed, or intimidating or coercing him or a third person, or for any reason based on discrimination of any kind" (Art. 1, Sec. 1). Moreover, the U.N. Convention explicitly states, "No exceptional circumstances whatsoever, whether a state of war or a threat of war, internal political instability or any other public emergency, may be invoked as a justification of torture" (Art. 2, Sec. 2).

This is why the testimony of Henri Alleg reverberates today. Alleg revealed to the French public that torture, once accepted in "exceptional" circumstances, becomes routine when the enemy is dehumanized in the ordinary daily practice of soldiering and policing. As Jean-Paul Sartre stresses in his essay, racial and religious superiority were the dominant themes behind French torture. "For most Europeans in Algeria . . . [the colonists] have the divine right, and the natives are sub-human." The Americans—soldiers, civilian contractors, intelligence agents, even doctors—torturing prisoners today in Cuba, Iraq, Afghanistan, Diego Garcia, and elsewhere are the heirs of that imperialist process.

Well before the U.S. invasion of Iraq, the U.S. Army screened for its officers Gillo Pontecorvo's famous 1965 film, *The Battle of Algiers*, as an example of urban guerrilla warfare in an Arab Muslim nation. The film is a vivid reenactment of the French army's method of brutally crushing the insurgency in Algiers in 1957, and shows the place of torture in its strategy.

What the public—then and now—does not know is that the sadistic methods of prisoner management are not the mistakes of a few ill-trained soldiers and other guards. They are the beginning of what has become generalized and systemic practice. The Bush administration may argue that torture "is not part of our culture." but the simple fact is that it is being used regularly.

From the president on down, our political, military, legal, and ethical authorities improvise justifications for torture as they go along, just as French leaders in the 1950s sententiously invoked everything from "Muslim terrorism" to "international communism" and the "threat to French civilization" as they outdid one another to downplay or justify what the troops were doing.

There is a long trail of precedents from France's imperial twilight to the present. French soldiers who honed their skills at torture in Indochina in the early 1950s and in Algeria a few years later were invited to Fort Bragg, North Carolina, in the early 1960s to train American GIs bound for Vietnam in their special methods of "interrogation." That the French had lost their wars apparently did not matter. American optimism trumped serious reflection on historical lessons. Torture was used as a matter of routine in Southeast Asia, in Latin America, in the Middle East. U.S.-sponsored death squads flourished in many countries.

In recent years, the United States has sought to revise the meaning of torture, limiting, if not eliminating, its illegality. There are efforts to redefine what is happening, to suggest that "torture lite" is not torture, or that "creative" or "aggressive" practices, even if torture, are necessary today in the "war on terror."

The administration and the Pentagon have issued numerous reports suggesting that the defenses of "necessity" and of "superior orders" may be invoked against charges of torture, despite the unequivocal language of the U.N. Convention and of the Nuremberg Principles. Moral standards are being manipulated, and both international and domestic law disregarded.

Military doctors, including psychiatrists, are an integral part of these operations. They advise the interrogators on new ways to be more successful in extracting information—true or false— in violation of the Geneva Conventions. Despite mounting evidence that information obtained through torture is notoriously unreliable, political justification leads to intellectual justification, and pressure is building to redefine the rule of law with respect to torture. They observe and report on torture sessions, in violation of the Declaration of the World Medical Association, to which the American Medical Association is a signatory. The effect is to assist in refining methods of inducing mental and physical pain in a chilling reversal of medical standards, trying to test the limits of what is permissible. One law professor representing a Guantanamo detainee told a *New Yorker* reporter, "The whole place appears to be one giant human experiment."

This medical complicity is not new. Technologies change, but strategies seldom do. Henri Alleg recounts how, during his three months of "treatments," doctors were assisting in the prison where he was held with the feared injections of "truth serum" and other medical ministrations.

The role of public opinion cannot be overemphasized. Henri Alleg contributed greatly to turning French public opinion against the war in Algeria and against continued French domination in Africa. His book and the writings of his supporters helped stop torture in Algeria. The ordinary French citizen was outraged.

But today in the United States we run the risk that the public has become anesthetized to what is happening. It is all so commonplace: so many photographs, so many investigations, one low-ranking GI court-martialed here, another there. And we are constantly reminded that anything is justified in the war against terrorism.

The moral rot that spread through France and French institutions finally brought down the Fourth Republic. Could increasingly brazen and desperate disregard for our own laws and procedures, as well as international conventions that we are pledged to obey, have a comparable effect on our society?

The United States will not accept the International Criminal Court for fear its soldiers might be prosecuted. As recently as June 2005 the *New York Times* worried that "red tape" must not hamper the interrogation of terrorists. The Geneva Conventions? The United Nations Convention Against Torture? Red tape? Has the public really become inured to it all? What does this do to the moral fabric of our society and to the individuals who order and perform such practices, and to those of us who merely shut our eyes to them?

It took hundreds of years for the prohibition of torture to become a part of international law. We should not let political opportunists reverse that, destroying what took humanity so long to establish.

The French methods in Algeria were not the excesses of a few rogue officers, and American politicians would do well to ask themselves whether, a few years from now, they will be blaming "rogue officers" for what happened in the war against terror, or whether Americans will be the defendants in future war crimes trials.

INTRODUCTION

James D. Le Sueur

How a democratic state ultimately accounts for its use of extreme violence during wartime reveals much about its political character. On this count, the French government has not generally scored high marks, especially regarding its military's liberal application of torture during its wars of decolonization. Indeed, the state's virtual inability to confront the legacy of colonial violence continues to serve as a matter of intense national debate and as a fruitful subject of inquiry. France's difficulty in responding to these questions is undoubtedly because torture was about as commonplace during the wars of decolonization as the impunity enjoyed by the state's paid assassins and torturers. But torture was never as prevalent, nor as glaringly unexamined by the French state, as in its brutal war against nationalists in Algeria (1954–62). Charles de Gaulle protected France's professional torturers from trial with successive waves of amnesty (by decree) beginning in 1962 (the last coming in 1968, when de Gaulle even amnestied his own would-be assassins in the infamous Organisation de l'Armée Secrète, or OAS) and thereby rendered it impossible to bring anyone involved in Algeria to court for crimes against humanity.

The price of this 1960s political maneuvering is clear: France has today settled into an uncomfortable postcolonial conundrum that forces it to fret over how the history of colonialism can be taught in the university curriculum. More to the point, as recently as February 2005, the French National Assembly responded to the political pressures applied by veterans, ex-colonials, and the *harkis* (Algerians who fought for France against their compatriots) with the passage of a controversial law calling for, among other things, teaching the "positive role" of French colonialism overseas and the military's "sacrifices," especially in North Africa.[1] Moreover, in the wake of the worst riots in France since 1968 and in the face of intense protest by leading French historians, the French parliament voted again on November 29, 2005, to uphold this revisionist law by a clear margin of 183 to 94. Henri Alleg's *The Question*, the stunning account of torture written by a French victim of military "interrogation" during the infamous Battle of Algiers, can once again serve English readers as a useful counterbalance to France's state-sanctioned amnesia and well-established ahistoricism regarding colonial violence. More importantly, it serves as evidence of the dehumanizing effects of torture on all parties.

Written in cell 72 in the Algiers prison four months after Alleg underwent weeks of brutal torture at the hands of the notorious Paras (French paratroopers), and published midway through Algeria's war of independence in 1958, *The Question* has the distinction of being the first book banned in France since the eighteenth century. Officially, it was banned because the French government considered it anticolonial communist propaganda. Unofficially, it was banned by the doomed French Fourth Republic (which was overthrown by a military coup d'état that illegally brought Charles de Gaulle back to power in May 1958) precisely because it ended the state's ability to deny that torture had become a preferred and practically universal method of interrogation in Algeria.

The simple fact is that French authorities tortured Algerians long before the beginning of the Algerian revolution, but Alleg's book moved "the question" (torture) fully into public view and immediately attracted the attention of many important writers and activists. The French philosopher Jean-Paul Sartre quickly added his moral weight to Alleg's text by penning a famous essay, "The Victory," for the Parisian magazine *L'Express*. Soon after, a new edition of *The Question* was published in French by Presses de la Cité in Lausanne, combining the two texts. This combined edition became the basis for the current English translation, which was published in the United States by George Braziller in 1958. Soon *The Question* was translated into Italian, Dutch, Japanese, Czech, German, Hungarian, Romanian, Polish, Russian, and other languages.[2] And now, almost fifty years later, it is available for the first time in this Bison Books edition.

Sartre, a staunch anticolonialist and supporter of the French Resistance during the Second World War, understood clearly the implications of Alleg's book and knew that France had already betrayed the very core values that had served the French Resistance so well in its combat against Nazi occupation. In fact, what pained Sartre the most was the ease with which those men who had been tortured by the Nazis could become Nazi-like torturers themselves. To be sure, this could happen in part because the French population swallowed the government's "ticking bomb" propaganda and incessant fear mongering. As Sartre put it, "If we must either terrorise or die ourselves by terror, why do we go to such lengths to live and to be patriots?" (14). But it was unfortunately also fueled, Sartre pointed out, by a species of colonial racism that had become an integral part of the mentality of mainland France.

Jean-Paul Sartre was, of course, not alone in France in criticizing the military's general use of torture during decolonization and more specifically against Alleg. In fact, hundreds of intellectuals and activists, including de Gaulle's own future minister of culture, André Malraux, and two Nobel laureates in literature, François Mauriac and Roger Martin du Gard, as well as some prominent military officers such as Gen. Jacques de Bollardière (who was censured for his criticisms), denounced the state for its torturing of Alleg. In this sense, Alleg's case galvanized French activists and intellectuals (Albert Camus was a glaring exception) and united them in their opposition to the violation of human rights in Algeria. In short, Alleg's famous book became the crucible for public protest against the French military's methods of ending the Algerian "insurrection." It is important to understand why this was so.

Because he was an important French writer and communist activist living in Algeria, French citizens could identify with him more than they could with Algerian nationalists undergoing similar horrors. He was the editor of a widely read Algiers independent leftist newspaper, the *Alger républicain*, which represented a strong anticolonialist position. The newspaper was banned by the French government in September 1955, an act that placed Alleg in peril. Following a pattern similar to that experienced by his Algerian counterparts, Alleg was eventually forced into hiding in November 1956 and was finally arrested in June 1957 by Gen. Jacques Massu's Tenth Paratrooper Division on charges that he had been involved in publishing banned material. He was first held in custody at the prison in El Biar for one month, during which he endured several intense torture sessions that he detailed to great effect. After that, he was transferred to a detention camp at Lodi. It was in the camp at Lodi that he began to write of his experiences, and it is this written account that was smuggled out of prison and eventually to France. It was banned about two weeks after it was published, but only after an estimated sixty thousand copies were sold.[3] Because of the banning, *The Question* was published in Switzerland and then smuggled back into France.

Throughout much of the time that this banned book was being read and debated in Europe and elsewhere, Henri Alleg remained in prison. French authorities kept him in prison in Algiers for three years, and then he was transferred to a prison in Rennes, France, in which he remained on trumped-up charges until his escape in October 1961, just months before the war ended in March 1962.[4]

Alleg's book is important for many reasons, but foremost among them is that it set off a chain reaction of protest by French citizens against the French state's prosecution of the war and more specifically against the misdeeds of the military—not unlike the fin-de-siècle Dreyfus Affair had. Written as a first-person account of victimization, it also illustrates that, as common as torture was, Alleg fully understood that his case was extraordinary in that—unlike many of the Algerians who endured even more sadistic acts in the French military and police torture chambers—his arrest provoked an immediate sense of outrage among the Europeans in mainland France. As he put it, "My particular case is exceptional in that it has attracted public attention. It is not in any way unique" (34). This account thus details his experiences as a European being "interrogated" by French military personnel using electric shock (including on his genitals), water torture, and beatings. He wrote: "I have survived so much pain and so many humiliations during this time that I would not bring myself to talk once again of those days and nights of agony if I did not believe that it would serve a purpose, and that by making the truth known I might do a little towards bringing about a cease-fire and peace" (34). His book was therefore a story of immense personal anguish and an attempt to make sure that the story of Algerians and others (including another Frenchman, Maurice Audin, who was disappeared in 1957 by the French military) reached the general public.[5] Muslim prisoners, Alleg is careful to point out, suffered far worse forms of torture than his own, and these crimes included the widespread raping of Muslim women by French soldiers.

By the time Alleg's book appeared in 1958, France had just begun to grasp the full extent of the human rights abuses in Algeria. In June 1957, the same month that Alleg was arrested, a French writer and Nuremburg POW, Pierre-Henri Simon, published an important book, *Contre la torture*. Simon's book offered one of the first major discussions of the problem of torture in the French military and served as a wakeup call to all those who denied that French soldiers used torture extensively in the Algerian conflict. More generally, the Algerian debates migrated to the United States when, in July 1957, Senator John F. Kennedy delivered his famous speech, "Imperialism—the Enemy of Freedom," on the Senate floor. He deplored the effects of the war in Algeria, and ever cautious, Kennedy warned that the war would weaken the French military's ability to live up to its NATO obligations. He pointed out that the government itself was on the verge of collapse. This led him to support Algerian nationalists' efforts to achieve self-determination via a federation with France.[6]

Yet within France itself, other publications continued to surface despite the state's extensive efforts to suppress them. One was *La Gangrène*, edited by Jerôme Lindon in June 1959, which detailed how the practice of torture had moved to the Paris prisons during the war. Finally, along with Alleg's case, another infamous case of torture involved Djamila Boupacha, a young Algerian woman who lost her virginity after she was tortured and raped by French soldiers with a beer bottle. Her case provoked international and domestic outrage in France in the early 1960s, when it was taken up by Simone de Beauvoir in a June 3, 1960, article in *Le Monde* and later chronicled by Gisèle Halimi and Simone de Beauvoir in a book entitled *Djamila Boupacha* (1962).[7] Not surprisingly, after his own escape from the prison in Rennes, Alleg came to Boupacha's defense with testimony he had written in exile about prison abuses in Algeria, which was published in the appendices of *Djamila Boupacha* and supported Boupacha's accusations against the French state.[8]

Alleg's escape, short time in exile, and eventual return to Algeria are themselves fascinating stories, ones that have recently come to life in his autobiography, *Mémoire algérienne*, and which merit a few words here. After his transfer to Rennes, Alleg's health quickly deteriorated because he had difficulty eating. He lost a considerable amount of weight, and at the insistence of the prison's doctor, he was admitted to the nearby hospital—where he was placed under armed guard, put in a padded cell, and given much-needed medical attention. However, as perhaps France's most famous political prisoner, Alleg's presence in Rennes did not go undetected, and he quickly discovered that he had well-placed allies in the local Communist Party cell who also happened to be employed at the hospital. After some planning, they were able to break him out, arrange for his false papers, and escort him safely across the French border into Switzerland. After an initial stopover in Geneva to recover his strength, he moved on to Czechoslovakia. While fleeing from French justice, he continued to meet important communist leaders, including Fidel Castro, but he remained eager to return to Algiers to work toward Algerian independence. Once the Evian Accords concluded the war in March 1962, Alleg planned a return to Algiers, but with the OAS continuing its fascist killing spree in Algeria, it remained unsafe. At the same time, during the violent and chaotic spring and summer of 1962, approximately one million pieds noirs returned to France in what was to be the largest single exodus of ex-colonials in modern world history.

Still a fugitive but in contact with the leadership of the National Liberation Front (FLN), Alleg continued to dream of his return to Algeria and of editing the *Alger républicain*, which had been out of publication since France banned it in 1955. Determined to return, he first resolved to go to Rennes to clear his name. One afternoon in May 1962, he simply knocked on his old prison's door. Stunned by Alleg's sudden reappearance, the guard who opened the door exchanged short pleasantries and then shut the door. Alleg knocked again and explained to the man that he had come to collect the things he left behind in October 1961 and asked to see the warden. Alleg then surrendered himself to police custody. The warden greeted him, asked him to wait, and made the appropriate calls. Soon, a telegram arrived from the office of the minister of justice ordering the judge in Rennes to drop the case entirely.

No longer a wanted man in France, Alleg was back in Algiers by midsummer 1962 once again editing the *Alger républicain* for post-independence Algeria. For the next three years Alleg lived in Algeria (a choice made by very few French citizens after independence), directed his newspaper in President Ahmed Ben Bella's independent Algeria, and worked alongside Algerian intellectuals to build a healthy discourse of democracy. However, Ben Bella was overthrown and put in prison during a military coup led by Houari Boumediene in June 1965. Boumediene's totalitarian approach immediately reintroduced censorship of the press, and for the second time in Algiers, Alleg found himself in the precarious position of being the editor of a banned newspaper, only this time by the very political party (the FLN) that he helped to liberate from France. Ironically, as Alleg himself points out in his memoirs, Algeria was the first government in the world to officially condemn the practice of torture in its own constitution, but it had begun to suppress all political dissent with the same violent methods used by the French during decolonization. [9] Fearing rearrest, torture, or worse, Alleg and many others were soon forced to return to France. Bitterly disillusioned with the failure of Boumediene's government to ensure democracy after independence, Henri Alleg continued to write in France. He went on to publish many important works, including his monumental three-volume set entitled *La Guerre d'Algérie* (1981), a retrospective discussion of *The Question* entitled *Retour sur "la Question": Entretien avec Gilles Martin* (2001), his commentary on American society and politics, *Requiem pour l'Oncle Sam* (1991), and his recently released *Mémoire algérienne* (2005). In 2002 he finally returned for a view of the building that once housed his office in Algiers.

In addition to his written work, Alleg has continued to apply pressure on the French state and veterans' groups to come clean about the use of torture, and for good reason. Although the French state has opened some of the archives on the French-Algerian war, it continues to block access to most of the sensitive files. According to French law (which is meant to protect privacy and does not only apply to state-related issues), sensitive records involving individuals can be withheld for up to one hundred years, which means that many of the Algerian files might not be made available to professional historians for several more decades.

The legal hurdles that postpone historical (but non-actionable) inquiries into potential war crimes by French officials during decolonization have caused some professional archivists to take matters into their own hands. For example, in one of the many spectacular twists arising from the Algerian conflict, Brigitte Lainé and Philippe Grand (both employed by the Archives de Paris), at great personal and professional risk, broke French law regulating the use of sensitive information when they released documents from the Paris police department's files supporting the defense of French historian Jean-Luc Einaudi. After Maurice Papon was convicted in 1997 for his activities as a Nazi collaborator during the Second World War, Papon filed a defamation suit against Einaudi, the author of the important 1991 book, *La Bataille de Paris (17 october 1961)*. Einaudi had claimed that Papon, who also directed the Prefet de Police during the Algerian conflict, had been involved in the terrible massacre of some three hundred Algerians by Paris police on October 17, 1961. Knowing that Papon's denials could be countered by out-of-reach evidence in the police archives, and risking a one-year jail sentence and fine of one hundred thousand French francs, in 1999 Lainé and Grand released documents that backed Einaudi's defense against Papon's defamation suit. Although not sentenced themselves, Lainé and Grand immediately lost their jobs. Among the more than 750 professional historians and activists from around the world who petitioned the French government for their reinstatement and for the release of more holdings were some of the most prominent intellectuals in France, including Pierre Vidal-Naquet and, not surprisingly, Henri Alleg himself.[10]

That said, there have been important developments, despite the state's best efforts to suppress the torture debates. The most infamous is that of Gen. Paul Aussaresses, the officer who ran the notorious secret service in Algiers and who developed many torture techniques. In reply to an interview published in *Le Monde* in 2000 in which an Algerian victim of torture, Louisette Ighilahriz, explained how she had been tortured by Massu's officers, the French generals offered their own responses.[11] General Massu finally apologized and admitted to excesses, Gen. Marcel Bigeard called her a liar, and General Aussaresses seized the moment to catapult himself from obscurity into the center of a political storm. In his own response to *Le Monde*, Aussaresses indicated that that he had personally killed twenty-four Algerian nationalists and that he did not regret his use of torture because it was done in order to protect innocent civilians in Algeria.

Knowing that he could not be prosecuted for his crimes, Aussaresses then published *The Battle of the Casbah: Terrorism and Counter-Terrorism in Algeria, 1955–1957* as an attempt to contextualize and justify torture and the technique of "disappearing" that he and General Bigeard perfected during the war in Algeria. Ironically, but consistent with the French state's position on Algeria, Aussaresses was not brought to trial for the crimes that he bragged about publicly (torture, murder, and disappearing) but for telling the story at all and technically for "justifying war crimes." Hence, in January 2002 he was fined 7,500 euros for publishing his book. In his book Aussaresses makes brief mention of Alleg's *The Question* and notes that the "Alleg and Audin cases became sensational in France because of the interpretation provided by the Communist Party and the newspapers supporting the FLN [National Liberation Front]."[12]

During the time that the Aussaresses scandal flared in Paris,

Henri Alleg publicly criticized the state's mishandling of the Aussaresses case, called for a stiffer treatment of former war criminals, and demanded (along with Pierre Vidal-Naquet and others) that Aussaresses and the French state account for the disappearance of Maurice Audin and thousands of still-missing Algerian nationalists. However, despite his misgivings about the French judicial process regarding amnesty for torturers, in an interview with the Algerian newspaper *Le Quotidien d'Oran* in January 2002, Alleg did point out one positive side to the Aussaresses trial, which otherwise had turned out to be a "cynical counter-apology for torture and summary executions." The positive dimension was that the case had introduced a number of French citizens "to what the war really was. The reality was always hidden from them."[13] The real problem President Jacques Chirac's government wanted to avoid, and which the Aussaresses case brought out, according to Alleg, was not the obvious one of bringing old torturers to trial but of condemning the various "civilian governments that had pursued its politics by encouraging these violent methods."

To be sure, after September 11, 2001, it has become all too clear that governments (perhaps especially that of the United States) can easily fall into uncomfortable conversations on the legality of torture. Furthermore, those very officers (including Aussaresses) who had overseen the use of torture and summary executions in Algeria during decolonization were also directly involved in the training of U.S. military personnel at Fort Bragg on counterinsurgency theory in the early 1960s and in the planning, along with U.S. personnel, of Operation Condor, a covert mission to eliminate left-wing opposition groups in Latin America. As presented in Marle-Monique Robin's 2003 documentary, *Death Squadrons: The French School*, the French government actively sent its professional torturers as official military advisors to the American military (to teach soldiers the elementals of counterinsurgency warfare techniques) and to the junta governments in Latin

America, including Argentina and Chile, whose reign of terror lasted for years. It is for this reason, perhaps, that Alleg's book also strikes an eerie resemblance to Jacobo Timerman's haunting book, *Prisoner without a Name, Cell without a Number* (1981), which is the autobiographical narrative of a Jewish Argentine journalist kidnapped in the late 1970s by the military and tortured for his publications critical of the military regime.

The fact that this edition of *The Question* comes out as the world confronts the sometimes blurred reality of torture in the post-September 11 world should at least give political leaders today reason to pause as they attempt to create ever more clever euphemisms such as "muscular questioning" to disguise the ugly truth about torture. The lessons of *The Question* remain as valid today as they were in 1958, and perhaps all the more so because the French question has now become a question for us all.

NOTES

I would like to thank Heather Lundine, Loukia K. Sarroub, David Schalk, and April Kirkendall for their help with this introduction. I am especially grateful to Lona Dearmont for her fine copyediting.

1. See Claude Liauzu, "Une loi contre l'historie," *Le Monde diplomatique*, April 28, 2005, 28.

2. Henri Alleg, *Mémoire algérienne* (Paris: Stock, 2005), 317.

3. Estimates on the precise number vary. I use the number most commonly accepted by historians.

4. Henri Alleg, interview by James D. Le Sueur, March 9, 1994, Paris.

5. Maurice Audin's case was taken up by Pierre Vidal-Naquet and Laurent Schwartz in their influential book entitled *L'Affair Audin* (Paris: Editions de Minuit, 1958).

6. For the full text of Kennedy's speech, see the *Congressional Record*, 85th Congress, 1st session, vol. 103, pt. 8 (June 21–July 10, 1957): 10781–10789.

7. For a longer discussion of Djamila Boupacha's case and others, see James D. Le Sueur, "Torture and the Decolonization of Algeria," in *Colonial and Postcolonial Incarceration*, ed. Graeme Harper (London: Continuum, 2001), and *Uncivil War: Intellectuals and Identity Politics during the Decolonization of Algeria*, 2nd ed. (Lincoln: University of Nebraska Press, 2005).

8. See "Testimonies" section for Henri Alleg's account written from the Rennes prison on September 9, 1961, in Gisèle Halimi and Simone de Beauvoir, *Djamila Boupacha, the Story of the Torture of a Young Algerian Girl which Shocked Liberal French Opinion* (New York: Macmillan, 1962), 203–7.

9. Alleg, *Mémoire algérienne*, 336.

10. See Jean-Pierre Thibaudat, "Deux archivistes toujours au placard," *Libération*, October 18, 2002, http://www.liberation.fr/page.php?Article =59514 (retrieved October 18, 2002).

11. For a more complete account of Louisette Ighilahriz's story, see her book, *L'Algerienne* (Paris: Fayard, 2001). Also see Adam Shatz, "The Torture of Algiers," in *The New York Review of Books*, November 21, 2002, and Le Sueur, *Uncivil War*.

12. Paul Aussaresses, *The Battle of the Casbah: Terrorism and Counter-Terrorism in Algeria, 1955–1957* (Enigma Books: New York, 2001), 158.

13. Arezki Benmokhtar, "Ce n'est qu'un début," Entretien avec Henri Alleg, après le process contre Aussaresses, *Le Quotidien d'Oran*, January 29, 2002, http://www.algeria-watch.org/farticle/1954-62/aussaresses_alleg .htm. (retrieved June 17, 2005).

PREFACE

'A VICTORY'

In 1943, in the Rue Lauriston (the Gestapo headquarters in Paris), Frenchmen were screaming in agony and pain: all France could hear them. In those days the outcome of the war was uncertain and the future unthinkable, but one thing seemed impossible in any circumstances: that one day men should be made to scream by those acting in our name.

There is no such word as impossible: in 1958, in Algiers, people are tortured regularly and systematically. Everyone, from M. Lacoste (Minister Resident for Algeria) to the farmers in Aveyron, knows this is so, but almost no one talks of it. At most a few thin voices trickle through the silence. France is almost as mute as during the Occupation, but then she had the excuse of being gagged.

Abroad, the conclusion has already been drawn: some people say our decline has gone on since 1939, others say since 1918. That is too simple. I find it hard to believe in the degradation of a people: I do believe in stagnation and stupor. During the war, when the English radio and the clandestine Press spoke of the massacre of Oradour, we watched the German soldiers walking inoffensively down the street, and would say to ourselves: 'They look like us. How can they act as they do?' And we were proud of ourselves for not understanding.

Today, we know there was nothing to understand. The decline has been gradual and imperceptible. But now when we raise our heads and look into the mirror we see an unfamiliar and hideous reflection: ourselves.

Appalled, the French are discovering this terrible truth: that if nothing can protect a nation against itself, neither its traditions nor its loyalties nor its laws, and if fifteen years are enough to transform victims into executioners, then its behaviour is not more than a matter of opportunity and occasion. Anybody, at any time, may equally find himself victim or executioner.

Happy are those who died without ever having had to ask themselves: 'If they tear out my fingernails, will I talk?' But even happier are others, barely out of their childhood, who have not had to ask themselves that *other* question: 'If my friends, fellow soldiers, and leaders tear out an enemy's fingernails in my presence, what will I do?'

The young conscripts driven to the wall by circumstances: what do they know of themselves? They sense that the resolutions they make here in France will, when they are faced with an unpredictable crisis, seem like empty abstractions. Alone and over there, they will have to take decisions for France and for themselves. After that experience they come home transformed, aware of their helplessness, and generally taking refuge in a bitter silence.

Fear is born. Fear of others and of themselves, and in France today fear permeates all sections of society. The victim and executioner merge into the same figure: a figure in our own likeness. In fact, in the final extremity, the only way to avoid one rôle is to accept the other.

This choice has not imposed itself—or at least not yet—on Frenchmen in France: but the indetermination weighs on us: because it has brought us near to the point where we may have to decide whether to be the torturer or the tortured: the horror of the one and the fear of the other drives us from one decision to the other. Old memories awaken; fifteen years ago the best members of the Resistance feared the suffering less than the possibility of their giving way under torture. Those who were silent saved the lives of all. Those who talked could not be blamed, even by those who did not give way. But the man who talks becomes one with his executioner. Coupled as man and wife, these two lovers made the abject night terrible. Now the terrible night has returned: at El Biar, it returns every night: in France, it is the ashes in our hearts. Whispered propaganda would have us believe that 'everybody talks', and this ignorance of humanity excuses torture. As every one of us is a potential traitor, the killer in each of us need feel no qualms. All the more so, as honeyed voices tell us every day that the glory of France demands it. The good patriot has a clear conscience, and only defeatists need be ashamed.

Suddenly, stupor turns to despair: if patriotism has to precipitate us into dishonour, if there is no precipice of inhumanity over which nations and men will not throw themselves, then, why, in fact, do we go to so much trouble to become, or to remain, men? Inhumanity is what we really want. But if this really is the truth, if we must either terrorise or die ourselves by terror, why do we go to such lengths to live and to be patriots?

These thoughts have given us strength; false and obscure, they all unravel from the same principle: that man is inhuman. Their purpose is to convince us of our impotence. They will descend on us if we do not face them squarely. We must let other nations abroad know that our silence is not an assent. It comes from nightmares which are forced on us, sustained and guided. I have known it for a long time and have been waiting for a decisive proof.

Here it is.

Two weeks ago a book was published by Editions de Minuit: *La Question*. The author, Henri Alleg, still in prison today in Algiers, tells without unnecessary padding and with admirable precision what he underwent when 'questioned'. The torturers, as they themselves promised, 'looked after' him: torture by electricity, by drowning as in the time of Brinvilliers, but with all the perfected technique of our own time, torture by fire, by thirst, etc. It is a book one would not advise for weak stomachs. Already the first edition—twenty thousand copies—is sold out; in spite of a second printing produced in haste, the publishers cannot satisfy the demand: some booksellers are selling fifty to a hundred copies a day.

xxx

Up to now it was only those returning from military service, particularly priests, who have been able to bear witness. They lived among the torturers, their brothers and ours. They knew of the victims principally by their screams, their wounds, their sufferings. They point to the sadists, bending over the torn flesh of their victims. And what distinguishes us from these sadists? Nothing does, because we do not protest: our indignation seems to us to be sincere, but would we be indignant if we had lived over there? Would we not have resigned ourselves to it instead? As for myself, I have to read by profession, I have books published, and I have always detested those books that involve us in a cause mercilessly and yet offer no hope or solution.

With the publication of *La Question*, everything is changed: Alleg has saved us from despair and shame because he is the victim himself and because he has conquered torture. This reversal is not without a certain sinister humour; it is in our name that he was victimised and because of him we regain a little of our pride: we are proud that he is French. The reader identifies himself with him passionately, he accompanies him to the extremity of his suffering; with him, alone and naked, he does not give way. Could the reader, could we, *if it happened to us*, do the same? That is another matter. What is important, however, is that the victim saves us in making us discover, as he discovered himself, that we have the ability and the duty to undergo anything.

We fascinate ourselves with the whirlpool of inhumanity; but it only needs a man, hard and stubborn, obstinately doing his duty to his fellow man, to save us from vertigo. The 'Question' is not inhuman; it is simply an ignoble and vicious crime, committed by men against man and that another man can and must rebuke. Inhumanity does not exist, except in the nightmares which engender fear. And it is just the calm courage of the victim, his modesty and his lucidity which wake us and show us the truth. Alleg underwent torture in the darkness of night; let us get closer, to look at it by daylight.

First of all, let us look at the torturers: who are they? Sadists? Fallen archangels? War lords with terrible caprices? If we are to believe them, they are all these things mixed up. But, quite properly, Alleg does not believe them. What emerges from the events he describes, is that they want to convince themselves and their victims of their invincible power: sometimes they present themselves as supermen who have other men at their mercy, and sometimes as men, strong and severe, who have been entrusted with the most obscene, ferocious, and cowardly of animals, the human animal. We know that they do not look at themselves very closely. The main thing is to make the prisoner feel that he does not belong to the same species: therefore they are undressed, they are beaten, they are mocked; soldiers come and go, proffering insults and threats with a nonchalance which they want to make as terrible as possible.

But Alleg, naked, trembling with cold, tied to a plank still black and sticky from the vomit of earlier victims, reduces all these things to their pitiable true nature: they are comedies played by fools. Comedy in the violent fascism of their nature, in the boast that they will 'blow up the republic'. Comedy in the persuasions of the '*aide de camp* of General M——', which finishes with these words: 'The only thing left for you to do is to kill yourself.' They are vulgar comedies flouting all conventions, renewed every night (without conviction) for all prisoners, and each session shortened for lack of time, because these horrible employments are overloaded with routine. Having been dragged in, prisoners have to wait in line to be attached to the torture plank; they are attached, detached, dragged from one torture chamber to another. In looking through Alleg's eyes at this unworldly hive, we see that the torturers are overloaded by their tasks.

They have their calmer moments, when they drink beer, relaxed, at the side of a tortured body, and then suddenly they jump to their feet, run around, curse and shout with rage; they are great neurotics who would make excellent victims; at the first electric shock they would tell everything.

Evil and savage they certainly are; sadistic they are not; they are in too much of a hurry. This is the one factor that saves them: they only keep themselves going by speed; if they lose impetus, they collapse.

Nevertheless they like work well done; if they think it necessary, they can push their professional conscience to murder. This is what strikes one most in Alleg's account: behind the haggard masks, we feel an inflexibility which

B

races ahead of them and which also races ahead of their masters.

We would almost be too lucky if these crimes were the work of savages: the truth is that torture makes torturers. These soldiers were not, after all, conscripted into an élite corps to martyr a defeated enemy.

Alleg in a few lines has described what he himself observed, and it is enough to mark the stages of a metamorphosis.

There are a few young ones, impotent, shocked, who murmur: 'It's horrible,' when their electric torch lights up a victim: and then there are the assistant torturers who do not as yet touch the victim with their hands, who carry and move the prisoners around, some of them hardened, others not, all caught up in the machinery, all of them already beyond forgiveness.

Then there is the young blond from the north: 'I looked at this youth with his sympathetic face, who could talk of the sessions of tortures I (Alleg) had undergone, as if it were a football match that he remembered, and could congratulate me without spite as he would a champion athlete . . . .' A few days later, Alleg sees him again 'shrivelled up and disfigured by hatred, hitting an Arab on the staircase . . . .' And there are the specialists, the hard ones who commit the atrocities, who take pleasure in the frenzied spasms of an electrocuted man, but who do not like to hear them scream; and then there are the lunatics who spin around like a dead leaf with the impetus of their own violence.

None of these men exist by themselves, not one of them will remain as he is: they all undergo a gradual transformation. Between the best and the worst, there is only one difference: the former are novices and the latter have been at it some time. They will all leave in turn, and if the war continues, others will replace them: these northern blonds and short, dark southerners, who have the same apprenticeship and find at the same time this taste for violence and its accompanying nervousness.

It is not the individuals, in this case, who matter. Executioners and victims alike are in the grip of a violent and anonymous hatred. It is a hatred that debases them both through each other, taking the form of torture and creating its own instruments.

Yet when this is said in the assembly, pretty timidly, the pack is let loose: 'You are insulting the Army!' These curs must be asked once and for all what this has got to do with the Army. Yes, torture *is used in the Army*, but what does this prove? The Commission de Sauvegarde, in a report which was in other respects benign enough, did not consider it necessary to hide the fact. After all, it is not the *Army* as such which does the torturing.

What folly! Do they think civilians do not know these excellent methods? If it were only a question of protecting the Army, why not co-operate with the Algiers Police? And then, if a chief executioner is all that is needed, the entire assembly will appoint one: it is not General S. less than General E., or even General M. who is named by Alleg: it is M. Lacoste, the man with absolute power.

All this happens next door to him, by his hand at Bône as at Oran: all these men who die of suffering and horror in the building at El-Biar, in the Villa S., die by his will. It is not I who say it is that way: it is the Deputies of the National Assembly, it is the Government. And the gangrene is spreading; it has crossed the sea: it has even got about that the 'Question' is applied in certain civil prisons in the Metropolis. I do not know if it has any foundation, but the persistence of the rumour must have troubled the authorities, because the prosecutor, in the trial of Ben Saddock, solemnly asked the accused if he had been submitted to torture; it goes without saying that the answer was known in advance.

Torture is neither civilian nor military, nor is it specifically French: it is a plague infecting our whole era. There are brutes East as well as West. One could cite Farkas, not so long ago torturing the Hungarians, and the Poles admitting that before the Poznan riots the police often used torture. The Khrushchev report shows conclusively what was happening in the Soviet Union when Stalin was alive. Men who only yesterday were being 'interrogated' in Nasser's prisons have subsequently been raised, still in a rather battered state, to high places. Today there is Cyprus and Algeria. In other words, Hitler was only a forerunner.

Disavowed—sometimes very quietly—but systematically practised behind a façade of democratic legality, torture has now acquired the status of a semi-clandestine institution. Does it always have the same causes? Certainly not: but everywhere it betrays the same sickness. But this is not our business. It is up to us to clean out our own backyard, and try to understand what has happened *to us*, the French.

How are the torturers justified? It is sometimes said that it is right to torture a man if his confession can save a hundred lives. This is nice hypocrisy. Alleg was no more a terrorist than Audin. The proof is that he was charged with 'endangering the safety of the State and reconstructing banned organisations'.

Was it to save lives that they scorched his nipples and pubic hair? No, they wanted to extract from him the address of the person who had hidden him. If he had talked, one more Communist would have been locked up, no more than that.

Arrests are made at random. Every Arab can be 'questioned' at will. The majority of the tortured say nothing because they have nothing to say unless, to avoid torture, they agree to bear false witness or confess to a crime they have not committed. As for those who do have something to say, we know very well that they do not talk. All of them or nearly all of them. Neither Audin, nor Alleg, nor Guerraudj unclenched their teeth. On this point the torturers of El-Biar are better informed than we. One of them said after Alleg's first session of questioning: 'All the same, he has gained a night to give his friends time to get away.' And one of the officers commented, a few days later: 'For ten years, fifteen years, they all have had the same idea, if taken they must not talk: and there is nothing we can do about it.'

Perhaps he was only talking about the Communists, but do we believe that the partisans of the A.L.N. are of a different metal? These tortures bring a poor return: the Germans themselves ended by realising this in 1944; torture costs human lives but does not save them.

In spite of that, the point is not altogether badly taken; it, at any rate, throws light on the function of torture: *the question*, that secret or semi-secret institution, is indissolubly allied to the secrecy of the resistance and the opposition.

Our Army is scattered all over Algeria. We have the men, the money and the arms. The rebels have nothing but the confidence and support of a large part of the population. It is we, in spite of ourselves, who have imposed this type of war—terrorism in the towns and ambushes in the country. With the disequilibrium in the forces, the F.L.N. has no other means of action. The ratio between our forces and theirs give them no option but to attack us by surprise: invisible, ungraspable, unexpected, they must strike and disappear, or be exterminated. The elusiveness of the enemy is the reason for our disquiet; a bomb is thrown in the street: a soldier wounded by a random shot: people rush up and then disperse: later, Moslems nearby claim they saw nothing. All this fits into the pattern of a popular war of the poor against the rich, with the rebel units depending on local support. That is why the regular Army and civilian powers have come to regard the destitute swarm of people as their uncountable and constant enemy. The occupying troops are baffled by the silence they themselves created: the rich feel hunted down by the uncommunicative poor. The 'forces of order', hindered by their own might, have no defence against guerillas except punitive expeditions and reprisals, and no defence against terrorism but terror. Everybody, everywhere, is hiding something: they must be *made to talk*.

Torture is senseless violence, born in fear. The purpose of it is to force from *one* tongue, amid its screams and its vomiting up of blood, the secret of *everything*. Senseless violence: whether the victim talks or whether he dies under his agony, the secret that he cannot tell is always somewhere else and out of reach. It is the executioner who becomes Sisyphus. If he puts *the question* at all, he will have to continue for ever.

But this silence, this fear, these always invisible and always present dangers, cannot fully explain the obsession of the torturers, their desire to reduce their victims to abjection and in its final stages their hatred of mankind which takes possession of them without their knowing it, and which fashions them into what they are.

It is normal for us to kill each other. Man has always struggled for his collective or individual interests. But in the case of torture, this strange contest of will, the ends seem to me to be radically different: the torturer pits himself against the tortured for his 'manhood' and the duel is fought as if it were not possible for both sides to belong to the human race.

The purpose of torture is not only to make a person talk, but to make him betray others. The victim must turn himself by his screams and by his submission into a lower animal, in the eyes of all and in his own eyes. His betrayal must destroy him and take away his human dignity. He who gives way under questioning is not only constrained from talking again, but is given a new status, that of a sub-man.

In Algeria the contradictions are irreconcilable. Each side demands the complete exclusion of the other. We have taken everything from the Arabs and now we have forbidden them everything even to the use of their own language. Memmi has already shown us how colonisation ends by the annihilation of the colonised. They own nothing, they are nothing. We have wiped out their civilisation while refusing them our own. They asked for integration and assimilation into our society and we refused. By what miracle could we continue to over-exploit the colonies if the colonised enjoyed the same rights as the colonisers? Undernourished, uneducated, unhappy, the system has mercilessly thrown them back to the confines of the Sahara, to the basic minimum of human subsistence. Under the constant pressure of their masters, their standard of living has been reduced year by year. When despair drove them to rebellion, these sub-men had the choice of starvation or of re-affirming their manhood against ours. They will reject all our values, our culture, which we believed to be so much superior, and it has become as one and the same goal for them to revindicate their claim to be men and to refuse our French nationality.

This rebellion is not merely challenging the power of the settlers, but their very being. For most Europeans in Algeria, there are two complementary and inseparable truths. That they have the divine right, and that the natives are sub-human. This is a mythical interpretation of a reality, since the riches of the one are built on the poverty of the other.

In this way exploitation puts the exploiter at the mercy of his victim, and the dependence itself begets racialism. It is a bitter and tragic fact that, for the Europeans in Algeria, being a man means first and foremost superiority to the Moslems. But what if the Moslem finds in his turn that his manood depends on equality with the settler? It is then that the European begins to feel his very existence diminished and cheapened.

It is not only the economic consequences of the emancipation of the 'wogs' that appall him but the implied threat to his own status as a human being. In his rage he may dream romantically of Genocide. But this is pure fantasy. Rationally he is aware of his need for the native proletariat to provide surplus labour, and chronic unemployment to allow him to fix his own wage rates.

Anyway, if he accepts the Moslems as human beings, there is no sense in killing them. The need is rather to humiliate them, to crush their pride and drag them down to animal level. The body may live, but the spirit must be killed. To train, discipline and chastise; these are the words which obsess them. Algeria cannot contain two human species, but requires a choice between them.

I am certainly not suggesting that the Algerian Europeans invented torture, nor even that they incited the authorities to practise it. On the contrary, it was the order of the day before we even noticed it. Torture was simply the expression of racial hatred. It is man himself that they want to destroy, with all his human qualities, his courage, his will, his intelligence, his loyalty—the very qualities that the coloniser claims for himself. But if the European eventually brings himself to hate his own face, it will be because it is reflected by an Arab.

In looking at these two indissoluble partnerships, the coloniser and the colonised, the executioner and his victim, we can see that the second is only an aspect of the first. And without any doubt the executioners are not the colonisers, nor are the colonisers the executioners. These latter are frequently young men from France who have lived twenty years of their life without ever having troubled themselves about the Algerian problem. But hate is a magnetic field: it has crossed over to them, corroded them and enslaved them.

It was thanks to Alleg's lucid calm that all this became apparent. We would be grateful to him if he had done nothing else. But in fact he did far more. By intimidating his torturers he won a victory for humanity against the lunatic violence of certain soldiers and against the racialism of the settlers. And what does this word 'victims' not evoke in terms of human tears, in the middle of these little cads, proud of their youth, their strength, their number? Alleg is the only really tough one, the only one who is really strong.

All we can say is something he never mentioned: that he paid the highest price for the simple right to remain a man among men. That is why this paragraph of his book is so moving. 'I suddenly felt proud and happy. I hadn't given in. I was now sure I could stand up to it if they started again, that I could hold out to the end, and that I wouldn't make their job easier by killing myself.' A tough one, yes, and one who, in the end, made the archangels of anger afraid.

In some respects at least we feel that the torturers can sense this and that they are expecting some nebulous and scandalous revelation. When the victim wins, then it is goodbye to their absolute power, their lordship. Their archangels' wings droop and they become just brutified men, asking themselves, 'And I, will I be able to take it too, when I am tortured?' Because in the moment of victory, one system of values is substituted for another; all it needs is that the torturers should become dizzy in their turn. But no, their heads are empty and their work keeps them too busy and then they only half-believe in what they are doing.

What is the point then in trying to trouble the consciences of the torturers? If one of them defaults, his chiefs will quickly replace him: one lost, ten found. Perhaps the greatest merit of Alleg's book is to dissipate our last illusions. We know now that it is not a question of punishing or re-educating certain individuals and that the Algerian war cannot be humanised. Torture is imposed by the circumstances and required by racial hatred; in some ways it is the essence of the conflict and expresses its deepest truth.

If we want to put an end to the atrocious and bleak cruelty, and save France from this disgrace and the Algerians from this hell, there has always been and still is only one way: to open negotiations and to make peace.

J.-P.S.

THE QUESTION

En attaquant les Français corrompus,
c'est la France que je défends.—JEAN-CHRISTOPHE

In this enormous prison, where each cell houses a quantity of human suffering, it is almost indecent to talk about oneself. The 'division' for those condemned to death is on the ground floor. There are eight of them in there, their ankles chained together, waiting for their reprieve or their end. And it is by the pulse of these condemned men that we all live. There is not one of them who does not turn on his straw mattress at night with the thought that the dawn may be sinister, who can fall asleep without wishing with all his force for nothing to happen at dawn. Yet it is from this section of the prison that the forbidden songs are heard every day, those magnificent melodies that always spring from the hearts of a people struggling for their freedom.

33

c

Torture? The word has been familiar to us all for a long time. Few of those imprisoned here have escaped it. The first questions put to new arrivals, when it is possible to speak to them, are these, and in this order: When were you arrested? Have you been tortured? By 'the Paras'* or the detectives?

My particular case is exceptional in that it has attracted public attention. It is not in any way unique. What I said in my petition and what I am saying here illustrates by one single example the common practice in this atrocious and bloody war.

It is now more than three months since I was arrested. I have survived so much pain and so many humiliations during this time that I would not bring myself to talk once again of those days and nights of agony if I did not believe that it would serve a purpose, and that by making the truth known I might do a little towards bringing about a cease-fire and peace. For whole nights during the course of a month I heard the screams of men being tortured, and their cries will resound for ever in my memory. I have seen prisoners thrown down from one floor to another who, stupefied by torture and beatings, could only manage to utter in Arabic the first words of an ancient prayer.

But, since then, I have come to know of other atrocities.

*Paratroops.

34

I have been told of the 'disappearance' of my friend Maurice Audin, arrested twenty-four hours before me, tortured by the same group who afterwards 'took me in hand'. He disappeared like Shiekh Tebessi, President of the Association of Oulamas, Doctor Cherif Zahar, and so many others. At Lodi, I met my friend De Milly, employed previously at the Psychiatric Hospital at Blida, who had also been tortured by the 'Paras', using a new technique: he was fastened down, naked, on a metal chair through which an electric current was passed; he still has the deep marks of severe burns on both legs. In the corridors of the prison I recognised among the new entries Mohamed Sefta, Registrar of the Mahakma of Algiers (the Moslem Court). 'Forty-three days with the Paras. Excuse me, but I still have trouble in speaking. They burnt my tongue.' And he showed me his slashed tongue. I have seen others: a young trader from the Casbah, Boualem Bahmed, showed me, in the prison car in which we were driven to the Military Tribunal, the long scars on the calves of his legs. 'The Paras . . . with a knife: I hid a member of the F.L.N.'*

On the other side of the wall, in the wing reserved for women, there are young girls of whom not one has given way: Djamila Bouhired, Elyette Loup, Nassima Hablal, Melika Khene, Lucie Coscas, Colette Gregoire and many others: undressed, beaten, insulted by sadistic torturers, they too have been submitted to the water and the electricity. Each one of us here knows of the martyrdom

*Front de Libération Nationale

of Annick Castel, raped by a parachutist and who, believing herself pregnant, thought only to die.

All this I know, have seen, have heard. Who can tell of all the other atrocities that I have not seen?

In reading these words you must think of all those who 'disappeared', of those, who sure of their cause, are awaiting their death without fear at this moment, of all those who have already been executed, of those who in the face of hatred and torture reaffirm their belief in future peace and friendship between the French and the Algerian peoples, because this book could be the account of each one of them.

IT was four o'clock in the afternoon of Wednesday, June 12th when Lieutenant Cha—— of the Paratroops, accompanied by one of his men and a policeman, arrived at Audin's house to arrest me. On the previous day my friend Maurice Audin, an assistant at the Faculty of Science of Algiers, had been arrested at his house and the police had left a detective behind. It was this man who opened the door to me when I fell into the trap. I tried, without success, to escape, but the detective, revolver in hand, caught me on the first floor and forced me into the apartment. The detective, who was very nervous, telephoned to Paratroop headquarters to ask for immediate reinforcements, watching me all the time out of the corner of his eye.

From the moment when the lieutenant entered the room I knew what to expect. Underneath an enormous beret, his small face, closely-shaven, triangular and long like that of a desert fox, gave me a tight-lipped smile. 'An excellent capture,' he said, enunciating each syllable.

'It's Henri Alleg, former editor of the *Alger Républicain.*'
Then turning immediately to me, he asked:

'Where have you been hiding?'

'That I won't tell you!'

He smiled, raised his head and then, very sure of
himself, said: 'We will prepare a little questionnaire for
you later on which will change your mind. You'll
answer, I promise you.' And then to the others: 'Hand-
cuff him!'

Escorted by the paras, I walked down the three flights
of stairs to the street. The lieutenant's car, an Aronde, was
waiting for us on the other side of the street. They made
me sit in the back. The Para was next to me: the barrel
of his sten-gun jarred against my ribs: 'There's a good
packet for you inside there, if you start any nonsense.'

We drove towards the higher part of the town. After
a short stop in front of a villa (without doubt one of the
communication posts of the Paratroops), where Cha——
entered alone, we continued to climb towards Chateau-
neuf by the Boulevard Clemenceau. Finally, after passing
the Place El-Biar, the car stopped in front of a large
building under construction.

I crossed a court filled with jeeps and military lorries
and arrived before the entrance of the unfinished building.
I went upstairs: Cha—— went ahead of me, the Para
behind me. The bars in the reinforced concrete stuck out

here and there from the masonry; the staircase did not have a balustrade; from the grey ceilings hung the wires of an unfinished electrical installation.

There was a constant movement of Paratroopers going up and down from one floor to another, pushing Arabs in front of them, prisoners dressed in rags with several-day-old beards, amid a great noise of boots, laughter and intermingled obscenities and insults. I was at the 'centre de tri'* of the sub-section of the Bouzareah. I was soon to learn how this 'tri' worked.

I went into a large room on the third or fourth floor behind Cha——, apparently the living room of a future apartment. There were several collapsible tables; blurred photographs of wanted suspects on the wall, which together with a field telephone made up all the furniture. Near the window stood a lieutenant. I learnt later that his name was Ir——. He had a great ape-like body, much too big for his small head with its sleepy eyes set between fat cheeks and for his little pointed voice which came out like the honeyed and spoilt tones of a vicious choirboy.

'We're going to give you a chance,' said Cha——, turning towards me. 'Here is paper and pencil. You're going to tell us where you live, who has been sheltering you since you went into hiding, who are the persons you've met, what your activities have been. . . .'

His tone was polite. The handcuffs had been taken off. I repeated for the two lieutenants what I had already said to Cha—— during the car journey: 'I went into hiding in

*Clearing Centre.

39

order not to be arrested because I knew that an intern-
ment order had been made out against me. I was looking
after the interests of my paper and I am still doing that.
On this subject I met M. Guy Mollet and M. Gérard
Jacques in Paris. I have nothing else to say to you. I shall
write nothing and don't count on me to betray those
who have had the courage to hide me.'

Still smiling and very sure of themselves, the two
lieutenants exchanged glances.

'I think there's no point in wasting our time,' said
Cha——. Ir—— agreed. At heart I, too, agreed with them:
if I was going to be tortured, it didn't matter very much
if it was earlier or later? And rather than being kept in
suspense, it was better to face the worst right away.

Cha—— went to the telephone. 'Get ready for a
session: it's a "prize catch" this time and tell Lo—— to
come up.' A few moments later Lo—— came into the
room. Twenty-five years old, short, sunburnt, pomaded
hair, small forehead. He came up to me, smiling, and
said, 'Ah! So you're the customer? Come with me.' I
went ahead of him. One floor further down I entered
a small room on the left of the corridor, the kitchen of the
future apartment. There was a sink, an earthenware
cooking stove, surmounted with a shelf on which the
tiles had not yet been laid and only the metal frame was in
place. At the back was a large glass door hidden by broken
boxes which darkened the room.

'Get undressed,' said Lo——, and, when I did not
obey him: 'If you don't we'll take them off by force.'

While I was undressing, Paras were coming and going all around me and in the corridor, curious to see who Lo——'s 'customer' was. One of them, a blond with a Parisian accent, put his head through the frame of the door where the glass had not yet been inserted and said: 'Well, a Frenchman! He's sided with the rats against us? You'll take care of him, won't you, Lo——!'

Lo—— now laid on the ground a black plank, sweating with humidity, polluted and sticky with vomit left, no doubt, by previous 'customers'.

'Lie down!' I laid myself down on the plank. Lo——, with the help of another, attached me by the wrists and ankles with leather straps fixed to the wood. I saw Lo—— standing above me, his legs apart, one foot on each side of the plank at the height of my chest with his hands on his hips in the attitude of a victor. He looked me straight in the eyes, trying to intimidate me like his superiors.

'Now listen,' he said, in his North African accent. 'The lieutenant is giving you time to think, but afterwards you'll talk. When we have a European we look after him better than the "wogs". Everybody talks. You'll have to tell us everything—and not only a little bit of the truth, but everything!'

During all this time I was being taunted by the 'blue berets' standing around me.

'Why don't your friends come and rescue you?'

'Well, well, what's he doing stretched out like that? Relaxing?'

Another one, more vicious, snarled: 'It's better not to

lose time with trash like that. I would show them the way things are right away.'

A current of cold air was blowing in from underneath the window. Naked on the damp plank, I started to tremble with cold. Lo—— insinuated with a smile: 'Are you afraid? Do you want to talk?'

'No, I'm not afraid. I'm cold.'

'You're still playing at heroes, are you? It won't last long. In a quarter of an hour, you'll talk very nicely.'

I remained in the middle of the paras who continued to joke and insult me, without answering, forcing myself to remain as calm as possible. Then I saw Cha——, Ir—— and a captain coming into the room. Tall, thin, with pinched lips, scarred cheek, elegant and taciturn, this was Captain De——.

'Well, have you thought about it?' It was Cha—— who put the question to me.

'I haven't changed my mind.'

'Good, we can proceed,' and addressing himself to the others: 'It would be better to go into the room next door. There's more light and it will be easier to work.'

Four Paras picked up the plank to which I was bound and carried me into the next room facing the kitchen, and put me down on the cement floor. The officers sat down around me on boxes brought in by their men. 'Now!' said Cha——, still very sure of the final result, 'I need some paper and a box, or something hard, to write on.' He was given a piece of wood which he put down beside him. Then, taking from Lo—— a magneto which the latter handed him, he raised it to the level of my eyes, turning for my inspection the machine which had already been described to me a hundred times by its victims. 'You know what this is, don't you? You've often heard it spoken about? You've even written articles about it?'

'You have no right to employ these methods.'

'You will see.'

'If you have any charge to bring against me, hand me over to the appropriate authorities. You have twenty-four hours in order to do it. And I would prefer not to be addressed as "tu".' There were bursts of laughter around me.

I knew very well that my protestations were useless and that under the circumstances it was ridiculous to ask these brutes to respect the law, but I wanted to show them that they had not intimidated me.

'Go ahead,' said Cha——.

A para sat on my chest: he was very sunburnt, his upper lip curled into a triangle under his nose with the broad smile of a boy who is going to play a good trick. . . . I was to recognise him later on in the office of the judge during my accusation. It was Sergeant Ja——. Another para (from Oran, to judge by his accent) was on my left, another by my feet, the officers all around me, and several others were also in the room without any particular function, but no doubt wanting to watch the fun.

43

Ja——, smiling all the time, dangled the clasps at the end of the electrodes before my eyes. These were little shining steel clips, elongated and toothed, what telephone engineers call 'crocodile' clips. He attached one of them to the lobe of my right ear and the other to a finger on the same side.

Suddenly, I leapt in my bonds and shouted with all my might. Cha—— had just sent a first electric charge through my body. A flash of lightning exploded next to my ear and I felt my heart racing in my breast. I struggled, screaming, and stiffened myself until the straps cut into my flesh. All the while the shocks controlled by Cha——, magneto in hand, followed each other without cease. To the same rhythm, Cha—— repeated a single question, hammering out the syllables: 'Where have you been hiding?'

Between two spasms, I turned my head towards him and said, 'You are wrong to do this. You will regret it!' Furious, Cha—— turned the knob on the magneto to its fullest extent.

'Every time you say that, I'll give you a packet!' And as I was continuing to scream, he said to Ja——: 'My God, he's noisy! Stuff his mouth with something!' Ja—— rolled my shirt into a ball and forced it into my mouth, after which the torture continued. I bit the material between my teeth with all my might and almost found some relief.

Suddenly, I felt as if a savage beast had torn the flesh from my body. Still smiling above me, Ja—— had attached the pincer to my penis. The shocks going through me were so strong that the straps holding me to the board came loose. They stopped to tie them again and we continued.

After a while the lieutenant took the place of Ja——. He had removed the wire from one of the pincers and fastened it down along the entire width of my chest. The whole of my body was shaking with nervous shocks, getting ever stronger in intensity, and the session went on interminably. They had thrown cold water over me in order to increase the intensity of the current, and between every two spasms I trembled with cold. All around me sitting on the packing cases, Cha—— and his friends emptied bottles of beer. I chewed on my gag to relieve the cramp which contorted my body. In vain.

At last they stopped. 'All right, untie him!' The first session was over.

I got up, reeling, and put on my trousers and my under-shirt. Ir—— was in front of me. My tie was on the table.

He picked it up and knotted it like a cord round my neck, and, amid the laughs of the others, dragged me off behind him, as he would have dragged a dog, into the office next door.

'Well,' he said, 'so you haven't had enough? We're not going to let you go. Get down on your knees!' With his enormous hands, he slapped me with his full strength. I fell on my knees, but I was incapable of keeping myself upright. I sagged sometimes to the left, sometimes to the right. The blows of Ir—— kept me from falling, except when he threw me down to the floor. 'Well, do you want to talk? You're finished, do you understand? You're a dead man living on borrowed time!'

'Bring in Audin,' said Cha——. 'He's in the other building.' Ir—— continued to hit me, while the other, sitting on a table, watched the spectacle.

My glasses had long since fallen off. My short-sightedness reinforced still more strongly the impression of unreality, of nightmare which had taken possession of me and against which I forced myself to struggle, lest it should weaken my will.

'Well, Audin, tell him what's in store for him. Save him from the horrors of yesterday evening!' It was Cha—— talking. Ir—— raised my head. Above me I saw the pale and haggard face of my friend Audin looking at me while I wavered on my knees. 'Go on, tell him,' said Cha——.

'It's hard, Henri,' Audin said to me. And they took him away.

Suddenly Ir—— pulled me up. He was beside himself. This was going on too long. 'Listen, you scum! You're finished! You're going to talk! Do you hear, you're going to talk!' He brought his face close to mine until it was almost touching and shouted: 'You're going to talk! Everybody talks here! We fought the war in Indo-China—that was enough to know your type. This is the Gestapo here! You know the Gestapo?' Then, with irony: 'So you wrote articles about torture, did you, you bastard! Very well! Now it's the tenth Paratroop Division who are doing it to you.' I heard the whole band of torturers laughing behind me. Ir—— hammered my face with blows and jabbed my stomach with his knee. 'What we are doing here, we will do in France. We will do it to your Duclos and your Mitterrand, we will do to them what we are doing to you. And your whore of a Republic, we will blow it up into the air, too! You're going to talk, I tell you.' On the table was a piece of hardboard. He picked it up and used it to beat me. Each blow stupefied me a little more, but at the same time confirmed me in my decision not to give way to these brutes who flattered themselves they were like the Gestapo.

'All right,' said Cha——. 'You've asked for it! We're going to throw you to the lions.' The 'lions' were those whose acquaintance I had already made, but who were going to exercise their talents still further.

Ir—— dragged me back into the first room, the one with the plank and the magneto. I just had time to see a

47

naked Moslem being lifted up amid kicks and pushed out into the corridor. While Ir——, Cha—— and the others were 'looking after' me, the rest of the group were continuing their 'work' using the same plank and the magneto. They had been 'questioning' a suspect in order not to lose any time.

Lo—— fastened me down to the plank: a new session of electrical torture began. 'This time, it's the big one,' he said. In the hands of my torturers I saw a different machine, larger than the first, and in my very agony I felt the difference in quality. Instead of the sharp and rapid spasms that seemed to tear my body in two, it was now a greater pain that took possession of all my muscles and tightened them in longer spasms. I was taut in my bonds. I tightened my teeth on the gag with all my might and kept my eyes closed. They stopped, but I continued to shake with nervous convulsions.

'Do you know how to swim?' said Lo——, bending over me. 'We're going to teach you. Take him to the tap!'

Together they picked up the plank to which I was still attached and carried me into the kitchen. Once there, they rested the top of the plank, where my head was, against the sink. Two or three Paras held the other end. The kitchen was lit only by a weak light from the corridor. In the gloom, I could just make out the faces of Ir——, Cha—— and Captain De——, who seemed to have taken over the direction of these operations. Lo—— fixed a rubber tube to the metal tap which shone just above my face. He wrapped my head in a rag, while De—— said to him: 'Put a wedge in his mouth.' With the rag already over my face, Lo—— held my nose. He tried to jam a piece of wood between my lips in such a way that I could not close my mouth or spit out the tube.

When everything was ready, he said to me: 'When you want to talk, all you have to do is move your fingers.' And he turned on the tap. The rag was soaked rapidly. Water flowed everywhere: in my mouth, in my nose, all over my face. But for a while I could still breathe in some small gulps of air. I tried, by contracting my throat, to take in as little water as possible and to resist suffocation by keeping air in my lungs for as long as I could. But I couldn't hold on for more than a few moments. I had the impression of drowning, and a terrible agony, that of death itself, took possession of me. In spite of myself, all the muscles of my body struggled uselessly to save myself from suffocation. In spite of myself, the fingers of my two hands shook uncontrollably. 'That's it! He's going to talk,' said a voice.

The water stopped running and they took away the rag. I was able to breathe. In the gloom, I saw the lieutenants and the captain, who, with a cigarette between his lips, was hitting my stomach with his fist to make me throw out the water I had swallowed. Befuddled by the air I was breathing, I hardly felt the blows. 'Well, then?' I remained silent. 'He's playing games with us! Put his head under again!'

This time I clenched my fists, forcing the nails into my

D

palm. I had decided I was not going to move my fingers again. It was better to die of asphyxiation right away. I feared to undergo again that terrible moment where I felt myself losing consciousness, while at the same time fighting with all my power not to die. I did not move my hands, but three times I knew again this insupportable agony. In extremis, they let me get my breath back while I threw up the water.

The last time, I lost consciousness.

On opening my eyes, it took me a few seconds to establish contact with reality. I was laid out, unbound and naked, in the middle of the paras. I saw Cha—— bending over me. 'It's all right,' he said to the others. 'He's coming round.' Then he addressed himself to me: 'You know, you did well to pass out. Don't think that you will always be able to lose consciousness . . . get up!' They propped me up. I staggered, leaning against the very uniforms of my torturers, ready to collapse at any moment. With blows and kicks they threw me like a ball from one to the other. I made a movement of defence. 'He's still got some reflexes—the pig,' one of them said.

'And now, what shall we do with him?' said another. Between their laughs I heard: 'We'll roast him.' 'Good. I haven't seen that yet.' It was Cha——, with the voice of somebody about to have a new experience.

They pushed me into the kitchen and there they made

me lie down on the stove and sink. Lo—— wound a wet rag around my ankles, which he then tied tightly with rope. Then altogether, they lifted me up in order to hang me head downward from the iron bar of the shelf above the sink. Only my fingers touched the ground. They amused themselves for a while, swinging me from one to the other like a sack of sand. I could see Lo——, who slowly lit a paper-torch at the level of my eyes. He stood up and all of a sudden I felt the flame on my penis and on my legs, the hairs crackling as they caught fire. I straightened myself with such a violent jerk that I bumped Lo——. He scorched me again, once, twice, then he started to burn me on the nipple of my breast.

But my reactions were now dulled and the officers moved off. Only Lo—— and one other stayed with me. From time to time they beat me or stepped on the extremities of my fingers with their boots as if to remind me of their presence. My eyes opened, I forced myself to look at them in order not to be taken by surprise with their blows, and in the moments of respite I tried to think of something other than the cords cutting into my ankles.

Then, from the corridor, two boots walked towards my face. I saw the upside-down visage of Cha——, who squatted in front of me, glowering furiously. 'Well, are you going to talk? You haven't changed your mind?' I looked at him and said nothing. 'Untie him.' Lo——

untied the rope which tied me to the bar while another pulled me by the arms. I fell flat on the cement. 'Get up!' I wasn't able to get up by myself. Held up on each side, I felt the soles of my feet swollen to the point where I had the impression that each step disappeared into a cloud. I put on my undershirt and my trousers, and, toppling over, fell all the way down a staircase.

There, another para picked me up and put my back against the wall, holding me up with both hands. I was trembling with cold and nervous exhaustion, my teeth were chattering. Lo——'s companion—the one who had 'looked after' me in the kitchen—had arrived on the landing. 'Move!' he said. He pushed me ahead of him and, with a kick, knocked me on the ground. 'Can't you see that he's groggy?' said another with a French accent. 'Leave him alone!' They were the first human words I had heard. 'Rats like that, they should be taken care of right away,' answered my torturer. I was trembling on my legs, and in order not to fall I put my palms and my forehead against the wall of the corridor. He pulled my hands behind my back and handcuffed them together, after which he threw me into a cell.

On my knees, I moved towards a mattress against the wall. I tried to lie on it on my stomach but it was stuffed inside with barbed wire. I heard a laugh behind the door: 'I put some barbed wire inside the mattress.' It was still the same man. Another voice answered him: 'All the same, he has gained a night for his friends to get away.'

The handcuffs were cutting into my flesh, my hands

hurt, and the position in which my arms were locked cramped my shoulders. I rubbed the tips of my fingers against the rough cement in order to make them bleed and take away a little of the pressure from my swollen hands, but I did not succeed.

From a small window, set high in the wall, I could see the night getting brighter. I heard a cock crowing and I estimated that the paratroopers and officers, tired by their night, would not come back before nine o'clock at the earliest; and that it was necessary for me to use all this time as best possible, in order to get back some strength before the next 'questioning'. Sometimes on one shoulder, sometimes on the other, I tried to relax, but my whole body refused to quieten down. I trembled constantly and was not able to find a moment of rest. I knocked several times against the door with my foot. At last someone came. 'What do you want?' I wanted to urinate. 'Piss on yourself,' he answered me from behind the partition.

It was already day when a paratrooper, the same one who had found the brutality of his colleague excessive, appeared and said to me: 'Come on, we're leaving.' He helped me to get up and supported me while I climbed the stairs.

They led me out on to an immense terrace. The sun was already very strong and from that point in the building one could see a whole quarter of El-Biar. From the descriptions which I had read, I realised right away that I was in the same building used by the paras, where Ali Boumendjel, Barrister at the Court of Appeal of Algiers had died. It was from this terrace that (as the torturers had given out) he had thrown himself in 'suicide'. We went down by another staircase into a different part of the building, where my gaoler locked me up in a small dark room. It was a dungeon, no bigger than a cupboard, where daylight never entered. Only a small narrow slit, situated high up in the wall and looking onto an air-vent, let a little light in. Crawling as best I could, I advanced towards a corner to support my back and give some relief to my shoulders which were contracted by cramp.

Very soon the traffic in the corridors became heavier. The building was waking up and I prepared myself for the return of my torturers. But Ir—— appeared all alone. He seized me by the shoulders to pull me up and led me to the landing. 'This is the man, Major,' he said. Before me was a major of the paratroops in camouflage uniform and blue beret. He was tall and ill-looking, extremely thin. In a soft ironical voice he asked me: 'You are a journalist? Then you should understand that we want to be informed. We must be informed.' He had only wanted to make my acquaintance: I was taken back to my cell. I did not stay alone for very long, for a few moments later Ir—— appeared. This time he was accompanied by Cha—— and by another para carrying a magneto. On the threshold of the door they looked at me: 'You still don't want to talk? You'd better realise that we'll go on with this to the end.' I was leaning against the wall facing the door. They came in, put the light on and settled themselves into a semi-circle around me.

'I need a gag,' said Cha——. He put his hand into one of the packages which were lying there and came out with a filthy towel.

'Don't bother,' said Ir——. 'He can shout as much as he wants, we're three floors underground.'

'All the same,' said Cha——, 'it's disagreeable.'

They unfastened my trousers, took down my underpants and attached the electrodes to each side of my groin. They took turns in manipulating the knob of the magneto —it was a large one of the second type used the previous day. I only cried out at the beginning of the shock and at each new wave of current and my movements were much less violent than during the previous sessions. They must have expected it, as they hadn't considered it necessary to tie me down to the plank. While the torture was going on I could hear a loud-speaker blaring out popular songs of the day. Without doubt the music was coming from a mess or common-room nearby. It largely drowned my cries and this was what Ir—— had meant by 'third floor underground'. The torture session continued and gradually exhausted me. I fell down, sometimes on the right, sometimes on the left. One of the two lieutenants detached one of the clasps and fastened it to my face until I jerked upright. 'My word,' said Cha——, 'he likes it.' They consulted together and decided they had better give me time to recover. 'Leave him the electric wires,' said Ir, 'as we're going to return.' They went away leaving the clasps still sticking into my flesh.

I must have fallen asleep suddenly, because, when I saw them again, I had the impression that only an instant had passed. And at this point, I lost all idea of time.

Ir—— was the first to come into the room. He gave me a kick, saying: 'Sit up!' I didn't move. They seized me and propped me up in an angle of the wall. A moment later I was writhing once again under the electric current. I felt that my resistance was making them more and more brutish and nervous.

'We'll give it to him in the mouth,' said Ir——. 'Open your mouth,' he commanded. In order to make me obey, he held my nostrils and the moment I opened my mouth to breathe, he pushed the naked wire as far in as he could, right to the back of the palate, while in the meantime Cha—— set the magneto in motion. I could feel the intensity of the current increasing, and my throat, my whole jaw, all the muscles of my face up to my eyelids contracting in a contortion that became more and more agonising.

It was Cha—— who was holding the wire now. 'You can let go,' Ir—— said to him. 'It will stay there by itself.' In fact, my jaws were soldered to the electrode by the current, and it was impossible for me to unlock my teeth, no matter what effort I made. My eyes, under their spasmed lids, were crossed with images of fire, and geometric luminous patterns flashed in front of them. I thought I could feel them being torn from their sockets by the shocks, as if pushed out from within. The current had reached its limit and so had my sufferings. The agony was constant and I thought that there was no greater harm they could do me. But I heard Ir—— say to the person who was working the magneto: 'Do it by little shocks: first you slow down then you start again . . . .' I felt the intensity diminish, the cramps which had stiffened my whole body decrease, and all of a sudden, as he turned the magneto back to its full force, the current was tearing me to pieces again. In order to escape these sudden easings and sharp increases towards the maximum agony, I started to bang my head against the ground with all my force and each blow brought me relief. Ir—— shouted into my ear at close quarters: 'Don't try to knock yourself out, you won't succeed.'

Finally they stopped. The flashes and points of light still danced in front of my eyes and my ears continued to buzz with the noise of a dentist's drill.

After a while I was able to distinguish all three standing up in front of me. 'Well?' said Cha——. I did not answer him.

'Good God!' said Ir——, and with all his force he slapped me.

'Listen,' said Cha——, rather calmer. 'Where can it get you—all this? If you won't say anything, we'll take your wife. Do you think she'll stand it?' Ir—— leaned over me in his turn and said: 'Do you think that your children are safe just because they're in France? We'll bring them here whenever we want.'

In this nightmare, it was only with the greatest difficulty that I was able to separate the menace I had to fear from the blackmailer's bluff. But I knew that they were capable of torturing Gilberte, as they had already tortured Gabrielle Giminez, Blanche Moine, Elyette Loup and other young women. I learnt later on that they had even tortured Madame Touri (the wife of a well-known Radio Algiers actor) in front of her husband, in order to make him talk. I was afraid that they would divine my anguish at the thought that they could effectively carry out their threats and it was almost with relief that I heard one of them say: 'He doesn't care, he just doesn't care about anything.'

They left me alone, but the idea that Gilberte might at any moment be attached to the torture plank could no longer be dispelled from my mind.

Cha—— came back a little later with another paratrooper. They tortured me once again and then left. I now had the impression that they were coming and going continually, only leaving me a few minutes of respite to recover. Cha—— tortured me again, moving the wire across my chest while continually rapping out the same question: 'Where did you spend the night before your arrest?' He put the photograph of one of the leaders of the Party, who had gone into hiding, under my eyes: 'Where is he?' I looked at Cha——, who this time was accompanied by Ir——. He was in civilian clothes, very elegant. I had to clear my throat, and he stepped away from me, saying: 'Look out! He's going to spit.'

'What does it matter to us?' one of the others asked.

'I don't like it, it's not hygienic.'

He was in a hurry and he was afraid of getting his suit dirty. He rose and left. I thought to myself that he had to go to some reception and that consequently at least one more day would pass from the time of my arrest. And I felt a sudden wave of joy at the thought that these brutes had not yet conquered me.

Ir—— also left, but I did not stay alone long. Into this obscure cell, they brought an Arab. The door opened for a moment, letting in a ray of light. I saw his silhouette: he was young and well-dressed; he had handcuffs on his wrists. He came forward, groping in the darkness and sat down next to me. From time to time I was shaken by fits of trembling and I would jump, groaning, as if the torture by electricity was still pursuing me. He felt me shaking and pulled my undershirt over my icy shoulders. He held me, so that I could get down on my knees and relieve myself against the wall, and then helped me to stretch out. 'Lie down, brother, lie down,' he said to me. I decided to say to him: 'I am Alleg, formerly editor of the *Alger Républicain*. Tell them outside, if you can, that I died here.' But I had to make the effort and there was not enough time. The door suddenly opened and I heard somebody in the corridor say: 'Why did they put him here?' And my Arab was taken away.

A little later the door opened again. This time it was two paras. An electric torch was shone on my face. I waited for the blows, but they never touched me. I was trying in vain to see who they were, but I only heard a young voice say: 'Horrible, isn't it?' and the other one answered: 'Yes, it's terrible.' And they went away.

Suddenly the electricity was switched on. It was two men from Ir——'s group. 'Hasn't he said anything yet?'

'Don't worry about it, in five minutes he's going to talk.'

'Ah!' said the second. 'You told your idea to the lieutenant?'

'Yes.' I understood that I was to learn new sufferings.

Ir—— appeared behind them. He leaned towards me, pulled me up and propped me against the wall. He opened my undershirt and stood facing me, his legs supporting mine, astride on the floor. He took out a box of matches from the pocket of his uniform, lit one and very slowly passed it in front of my eyes to see if they followed the flame, and if I was afraid. Then, using his matches he set about burning the nipple first of one breast, then the other.

He addressed one of his assistants. 'You can go ahead!'

This one then lit the paper torches which he had been

holding in readiness and started to scorch the soles of my feet. I didn't move and made no sound: I had become completely insensitive, and while Ir——— burnt me I was able to look straight at him without blinking. Furious, he hit me in the stomach and shouted: 'You're finished! Finished! Do you hear? Can you talk? I'll make you shit! You'd like me to kill you right away, wouldn't you? But it's not finished yet. Do you know what thirst is? We're going to let you die of thirst!'

The current had completely dehydrated my tongue, my lips, my throat, which were as rough and hard as wood. Ir——— must have known that torture by electricity induced an insupportable thirst. He had given up his matches, and in his hand he held a glass and a zinc jug. 'It's two days since you've had anything to drink. Another four days before you die of thirst. Four days can be a long time! You'll want to lick up your piss.' He poured a stream of water into the glass in front of my eyes and whispered into my ear: 'Talk and you can drink ... talk and you can drink.' With the rim of the glass, he forced my lips open. He had only left a finger of water in it and I could see the clear liquid moving at the bottom, but I was unable to drink a drop. His face close to mine, Ir——— laughed at my exhausted efforts. 'Tell the boys to come and see the torture of Tantalus,' he joked. Other paras were looking in the open doorway, and in spite of the fatigue against which I was fighting, I raised my head and refused to look at the water so as not to make my suffering an entertainment for these brutes.

'Oh, we're not as bad as all that. We'll let you drink all the same.' And he raised to my lips the glass which he had filled to the brim. I hesitated a moment; then, holding my nose and pushing my head back, he poured the whole glass down my throat: it was atrociously vile, filthy water.

Minutes or perhaps hours later there was a new interruption. De——, the captain, appeared in turn. With him was Lo——, Ir—— and the big paratrooper who took part in Wednesday's session. They propped me up against the wall and Lo—— attached the clips to my ear and my finger. At each shock I started but without crying out, having become almost as insensitive as a machine. De—— made a sign for them to stop.

Sitting on a packing-case, almost at ground level, he smoked and talked in a very soft voice which contrasted with the sharp tones of the others and their shouts, which still rang in my ear. He joked about subjects of no apparent importance and without any reference to the questions which had been hammered into my head since the beginning. Among other things, he asked me if many newspapers belonged to the French Press Federation. I would certainly have answered him, but I could not move my dry hard lips except with the greatest effort and only a dry whistle came out of my throat. Painfully, I tried to articulate certain syllables, while he went on talking as if one question was connected with the next: 'And Audin, he's a good friend of yours, isn't he?' This was like an alarm signal: I saw that he wanted to lead me on gradually, without realising it, to talk of something that interested him. Stupefied as I was by the blows and the tortures I had undergone, one single idea was still clear in my mind: 'Tell them nothing, don't help them in any way.' I didn't open my mouth.

At this, De—— lost his calm: he got up and started to hit me in the face with both fists. My head bounced from one side to the other to the rhythm of his blows, but I had lost all feeling, to the point where I no longer closed my eyes when his hand came towards me. He stopped after a while to ask them to bring him some water. 'We've already tried that, sir,' said Ir——. All the same, he took the glass and the jug that they handed to him. As the lieutenant had done earlier, he started to pour the water from one vessel to the other in front of my eyes, bringing the glass to my lips, but so that I could not drink it, but discouraged by my lack of reaction, because I made no effort to drink, he put it on the ground. I fell to one side. In my fall I knocked over the glass. 'Better mop it up,' said Ir——, 'or he'll lick it up.'

De—— having gone away, Ir—— took over in turn and with his sharp voice started to scream, bending over me: 'You're finished! This is your last chance! Your last chance! That's why the captain was here.' A paratrooper who had come in with Lo—— was sitting cross-legged in a corner. He had taken out his revolver and he was now examining it in silence, ostensibly to make sure that everything was in readiness. Then he put it on his knees as if waiting for an order. During this time, Lo—— had

connected the clips to me again and he worked the magneto by little jerks, but without conviction. I jumped
at each shock, but I was more worried about something
else. I seemed to see, lying on the ground against the
wall, an enormous pair of pincers wrapped in paper, and
I tried to imagine what new tortures were in store for me.
I thought that with this instrument they could perhaps
tear out my finger-nails: I was even rather astonished that
I felt so little fear and almost reassured myself with the
thought that my hands had only ten nails. When they had
finished and the door was closed, I crept towards the wall
and saw that the pincers were nothing more than a piece
of drainpipe sticking out of the masonry. It had become
more and more difficult for me to think without fever
dragging me back into unreality, but I felt that I could
not go on much longer. Memories of old tags kept
coming to my mind: 'The machine cannot go on for-
ever: the moment must come when the heart gives up.'
It was in this way that my young friend Djegri had died
two months earlier in a dungeon of the Villa S——, the
domaine of the 'Green Berets' of Captain Fau——.

When, some considerable time later, the door opened
again, I saw Ir—— come in, accompanied by two
officers whom I had not seen before. In the semi-darkness
one of them crouched down before me and put his hand

on my shoulder, as if to inspire confidence: 'I am the *aide de camp* of General M——.' It was Lieutenant Ma——. 'It grieves me to see you in this state. You are only thirty-six years old: that's young to die.' He turned towards the two others and asked them to leave. 'He wants to talk to me alone,' he explained. The door closed again and the two of us were alone.

'You're afraid that they'll know you talked? Nobody will know and we will take you under our protection. Tell me everything that you know and I will have you taken immediately to the infirmary. In a week you will be in France with your wife. You have our word. If not, you will disappear.'

He waited for a reply. The only one which came to mind, I gave him: 'Too bad!'

'You have children,' he went on. 'I could perhaps see them; do you want me to tell them that I knew their father? . . . You won't talk. If you let me go away now, the others will come back. And this time they won't stop.'

I remained silent. He got up, but before leaving, he said, 'There is nothing left for you to do but to kill yourself.'

I heard him exchange a few words with the others who were waiting for him in the corridor: 'For ten years, fifteen years they've all had the same idea, that if captured they must say nothing: and there is no way to change them.' I felt that I had arrived at the end of one stage of my ordeal: in fact shortly afterwards two paras came in.

They untied my hands, helped me to stand up, and then conducted me, supporting me all the time, to the terrace. Every second or third step, they stopped to enable me to get my breath back. In the passage other paras, standing around the stairs or on the landings, taunted them: 'Do you have to carry him? Can't he walk alone?' One of my guides answered them as if making an excuse, 'It's because he's had twelve hours grilling.' Then we went down into the other building.

AT the end of the corridor, I was taken into a cell on the left-hand side: this was in fact a bathroom not yet fitted up. One of the paras took me by the knees, the other under the arms and they put me on a mattress thrown against the wall. I heard them debating for a moment whether or not to put the handcuffs on me. 'He can hardly move; there's no point.' The other did not agree: 'We would be taking a risk we might regret.' Finally they attached my wrists, not behind my back, but this time in front. I had the most extraordinary sensation of relief.

High up on the wall, on the right, the lights of the town lit the room feebly through a small window, quartered by barbed wire. It was evening. Pieces of plaster had come loose on the ceiling and cracks had run down the rough cement of the walls. My fever turned these into living forms, half seen, all mixed up together. In spite of my exhaustion, I was unable to sleep: I was shaken by nervous trembling and the dazzle tired my eyes painfully. In the corridor they were talking about me: 'Give him a little to drink, a very little every hour, not much or he'll collapse.'

One of the paratroopers who had accompanied me, a young man with a French accent, came in with a blanket which he put over me. He made me drink: I swallowed a little, but I felt no thirst. 'Doesn't it interest you, the proposition of General M——?' he said. His voice was not hostile. 'Why are you so determined not to talk? You don't want to betray your friends? You have to have courage to hold out like that.' I asked him what day it was. It was Friday night, and they had started to torture me on Wednesday.

In the corridor was an incessant noise of steps and shouts, broken from time to time by the shrill voice of Ir—— giving orders. And suddenly, I heard terrible screams, very near by, probably in the next room. Somebody who was being tortured. A woman. And I thought I recognised the voice of Gilberte. It was only several days later that I knew I had been mistaken.

The torture went on until dawn, or very nearly. Through the partition, I could hear shouts and cries, muffled by the gag, and curses and blows. I soon knew that it was in no way an exceptional night, but the routine of the building. The cries of suffering were part of the familiar noises of the "Centre de Tri". None of the paras paid any attention to it, but I don't believe that there was a single prisoner who did not, like myself, cry from hatred and humiliation on hearing the screams of the tortured for the first time.

I was half conscious. I didn't really get to sleep until morning and woke up very late when the para of the previous evening brought me some hot soup: my first meal since Wednesday. I swallowed a few spoonfuls with great difficulty: my lips, my tongue, my palate were still extremely inflamed from the burns of the electric wires. My other wounds, the burns on my groin, my chest, my fingers, were infected. The para took off my handcuffs and I realised that I was unable to use my left hand, which was stiff and without any feeling. My right shoulder was extremely painful and did not allow me to raise my arm.

It was in the afternoon that I first saw my torturers again. I had the impression that they had agreed to meet in my cell. They were all there: soldiers, officers and two civilians (of the DST* without doubt) whom I had not previously seen. They started to talk among themselves, as if I were not present.

'So he doesn't want to talk?' one of the civilians said.

'We have time,' said the major. 'They're all like that at the beginning. We'll take a month, two months, or three months, but he'll talk.'

'He's the same type as Akkache or Elyette Loup,' answered the other. 'What he wants is to be a hero, and have a little plaque on a wall in a few hundred years.' He laughed at his joke.

*Direction de la Sûrêté de Territoire.

Turning towards me, he told me, smiling: 'We looked after you well.'

'It's his own fault,' said Cha——.

'He doesn't care about anything,' Ir—— said. 'He doesn't care about his wife or his children; he only cares for the Party.'

He had rested his foot on top of me as on a dead animal; then he announced, as if it had only just occurred to him: 'You know that your children are arriving tonight by plane? They're going to have an accident.' They started to go out, but De—— and Cha——, who had felt that I hesitated to take this blackmail seriously, lingered in the doorway:

'Don't you really care what happens to your children?' said the lieutenant. They waited a moment in silence and Cha—— concluded:

'Good! Then, you will die.'

'Everybody will know how I died,' I said to him.

'No, nobody will know anything.'

'Yes,' I said to him again. 'Everybody always knows.'

He had to come back the following day, which was Sunday, with Ir——, but only for a moment. The two of them were smiling. 'You haven't changed your mind?' Cha—— asked me. 'Then you are preparing new troubles for yourself. We have scientific ways (he emphasised the adjective) to make you talk.'

When they were gone, I knocked on the door and asked to be helped up. Supported by a para, I went to the kitchen and, leaning myself against the wall, splashed some water over my face. When I had lain down again, another para—this same European-Algerian who belonged to Lo——'s group—put his head through the half-open door and asked me in a mocking voice: 'Well, feeling better?'

'Yes,' I said to him in the same tone, 'you'll soon be able to start on me again.' I would have liked him to go on jabbering for a bit, as he might have given me a clue to what was in store for me, and what the "scientific" means were to be. But he only answered with spite: 'You're right, it's not finished. We'll open your mouth.'

It was Monday afternoon when Ir—— woke me. Two paras helped me to my feet and the four of us went down the stairs. One floor down was the infirmary: a large room with many windows; there were several camp beds and a table overflowing with medical supplies in complete disorder. The only person there for the moment was a military doctor, a captain, who seemed to be waiting for me. He was quite young, thin, with a dark skin badly shaven, his uniform torn. With his southern French accent he asked me, in place of greeting:

'Are you afraid?'

'No,' I said to him.

'I shall not beat you and I promise not to do you any harm.'

They laid me out on one of the camp beds. Bent over me, he took my pulse and ran over me with his stethoscope. 'We can go ahead. He's just a bit nervous,' he said to Ir——. I was upset that he had discovered my feelings in this way through my heart-beats. All these preparations confirmed my apprehensions. They were going to experiment on me with "truth drugs". These were the "scientific means" of which Cha—— had spoken.

Since the previous day, I had tried to remember everything I had ever read in the papers about pentothal. 'If the will-power of the patient is strong enough, he cannot be forced to say what he does not want to.' This was my conclusion, which I repeated to myself in order to keep calm and confident. It could not in any way help to defeat me: they had tied me down, and it was preferable to use all my energy to resist the drugs as best I could.

They waited a moment for the hospital attendant (or medical assistant) to arrive. He was coming back, no doubt, from an operation or a patrol, because he was dressed in campaign uniform. He took off his sten-gun and his equipment before listening to the doctor's explanations: 'First of all use five-centimetre cubes only, because there are some people who are immune.' He was thinking of the difficulty some people have in absorbing drugs, but at this moment I thought that he meant psychological resistance and I decided to give them the impression of not resisting. I thought it was the best way to get off with the smallest possible dose of the drug.

I was shaking with cold and nerves: I was naked to the waist, because my shirt, which no doubt somebody else had found to their taste, had never been given back to me. One of the paras threw a blanket over me and the attendant come up to me. He took my right arm, tightened the vein with a piece of rubber and plunged in the needle. Underneath the blanket I slid my left hand, stiff and numb, into the pocket of my trousers and, through the cloth, pressed it against my thigh, forcing myself to think that as long as I felt the contact, I would know I was not dreaming and would be able to remain on guard. The attendant only pressed very slowly on the syringe and the liquid entered my bloodstream drop by drop. 'Count slowly,' the doctor said to me. 'Start now!'

I counted: 'One, two, three . . .' until ten and then I stopped as if I were already asleep. At the base of my skull I felt a frozen numbness which mounted to my head and pushed me into unconsciousness. 'One, two, three,' said the doctor to encourage me. 'Continue.' I repeated after him: 'Fourteen . . . fifteen . . . sixteen . . .' I missed out on purpose two or three numbers, continued at nineteen, twenty and twenty-one and was silent. I heard him say: 'The other arm now.' Under the blanket, I slowly moved my right hand in order to put it in my pocket, always with the same idea that as long as my nails pinched my flesh, I would remain anchored to reality. But in spite of all my efforts, I fell asleep . . .

The doctor gently patted my cheeks. Almost whispering, he said to me in a voice that he tried to make as friendly as possible: 'Henri! Henri! It's Marcel; are you all right?' I opened my eyes. Slowly, with a great effort, I became aware of what was happening. It was dark in the room, he had pulled the blinds. Around me, sitting on camp beds, were paras and officers—those that I knew and others, who, no doubt, had been brought in to watch the experiment—listening in silence. I saw that the doctor had a piece of paper in his hand and understood that it was a list of questions he wanted to ask me.

In the familiar voice of someone who greets an old friend, he started by asking me: 'Have you been working long for the *Alger Républicain*?' The question was harmless: probably intended to put me at ease. I heard myself answering with extraordinary ease: I gave details of the difficulties of production on a newspaper, then I went on to describe how the pages were made up. I felt drunk, as if somebody else was talking in my place, but I had enough consciousness to remember that I was in the hands of my torturers and that they were trying to make me denounce my friends.

All this was no more than an introduction. The doctor whispered to his assistant: 'It's working, you see; that's the way to do it.' He broke into the middle of my explanations and said to me in a low voice: 'Henri, I've been told to come to you in order to see X——. What shall I do?' Under this friendly guise, was the same question that had been put to me twenty times under torture. A thousand pictures came into my befuddled mind: I was in the street, in an apartment, in a square and always with this "Marcel" who was pursuing me and plying me with questions. I made a great effort and, forcing open my eyelids, I managed to get a grip on reality long enough to plunge myself back again into semi-unconsciousness. He shook me a little to make me answer:

'Where is X——?' and a lunatic dialogue ensued.

'I'm astonished,' I answered him, 'that you've been sent to me. I don't know where he is.'

'When he wants to see you, how does he go about it?'

'He never needs to see me. I have nothing to do with him.'

'Yes, of course, but if he did want to see you, how would he go about it?'

'No doubt he would write to me, but he has no reason to do so.'

I was making a great effort in this cautious conversation, being sufficiently master of myself, in spite of the drug, to resist these brutes.

'Listen,' he went on. 'I have a soft job for X——. I have to see him urgently. If you see him, can you put me in touch with him?'

'I can promise you nothing,' I said to him. 'I would be astonished if he wanted to meet me.'

'Good; but if by chance he came, how could I get in touch with you?'

'Where do you live?' I asked him.

'26, Rue Michelet, 3rd floor on the right. Ask for Marcel.'

'Very well,' I said to him, 'I will remember the address.'

'No, that's not the best way: I gave you my address,

you should give me yours. You must have confidence
in me.'

'Well, then,' I said to him again, 'if you like, we can
meet at Parc de Galland Station in two weeks time at six
o'clock. I have to go now. I don't like loitering about in
the street.'

'Do you live near the Parc de Galland? Tell me your
address,' he said to me again.

I was exhausted and I wanted to bring the conversation
to an end, even rudely:

'You're wasting my time,' I said to him. 'Goodbye.'

'Goodbye,' he said.

He waited a moment, without doubt to ascertain that
I was fast asleep, and I heard him whispering to someone
near me: 'He won't say any more.' Then I heard them all
getting up and filing towards the door, as if after a show.
One of them, in passing, turned on the electric light, and
all of a sudden I was entirely conscious. They were all
by the door, some of them already outside, others,
including Ir—— and Cha——, still in the room and
looking at me. As loud as I could, I shouted at them,
'You can bring back your magneto! I'm ready for you!
I'm not afraid of you!' The doctor, a little bag in his
hand, went out, too: he signalled to them not to answer.
Before leaving the room, he said to the attendant: 'He
will probably be a bit difficult now. Give him some pills.'

Before the two paras who had brought me there took
charge of me again, the attendant dressed my wounds and
covered the burns on my hips and chest with adhesive

bandages. Then they helped me to return to my cell. One of the two, taking two pills out of his pocket, said to me: 'Swallow that!' I took them, slid them under my tongue, drank a mouthful of water and said to him: 'All right.' As soon as the door was closed I spat them out. Probably they were only aspirin tablets, but I was no longer able to think clearly and I felt myself filled with a sharp defiance of everything. Most of all I asked myself if this might not be the beginning of a "treatment". I felt that I was not in my normal state: my heart, my pulses were racing feverishly. I had a meeting with "Marcel". This pentothal phantom took on the reality of flesh and blood. I had succeeded in not answering his questions, but how would I defeat him the second time? I knew that I was in delirium. I struck and pinched myself in order to be certain I was not dreaming. But every time I returned to reality, I was unable to allay the fears that the drug had raised in me.

'Come on, we're moving!' It was my two guides from the infirmary. It must have been quite late, perhaps eleven at night, and as we climbed up to the terrace the idea came to me that they were going to make me "commit suicide". In the state in which I found myself, this thought did not cause me any additional emotion: 'I had not given way under torture, the serum hadn't worked, this was the end.' But we went down again into the second building and they opened the door of the dungeon where I had been before. It had been cleaned; there was a camp bed in it now, and a straw mattress.

As soon as they were gone, the same thoughts, put out of mind by this diversion, assailed me once again.

I asked myself if I was not going mad. If they continued to drug me, would I still be able to resist as I had done the first time? And if the pentothal made me say what I didn't want to, my agony under torture would have been for nothing.

The door of the cupboard on the right was open and I could see a roll of copper wire inside it. The open window above me had the hook of the latch left free. I could have attached the end of the wire to it, climbed on the camp bed and at the right moment pushed it away with a kick. But the idea of suicide revolted me. They would think after my death that it was the fear of torture which had driven me to it. I also asked myself if these "facilities" had not been placed there on purpose, and the words of the *aide de camp* of M—— came back to me: 'There is nothing left for you to do but kill yourself.' And at the very instant when I had decided not to kill myself, saying that if I had to die it was better to do so under the blows of the paras, I also asked myself if it was not perhaps the fear of approaching death which had put these arguments into my head. Death was death. Wasn't it better to die right away without the help of my executioners? I tried to make a decision as calmly as possible and I decided that in any case they would not come back for me before the following morning at least, that I still had sufficient time to kill myself if necessary. I also realised that I was not in a normal state and that I needed to sleep in order to think better.

I slept until morning. The night had taken away both my fever and my fears of the day before. I suddenly felt proud and happy not to have given way. I was convinced that I could still hold out if they started again, that I would fight them to the end, that I would not help them in their job of killing me.

Towards the middle of the afternoon, I was taken back to my first cell in the other building, but I did not stay there long. At night, I was taken back again and put into the dungeon, where I spent a second night. The snatches of conversation which I had picked up in the corridor gave me the explanation of these orders and counter-orders: they were waiting for the visit of a commission (I didn't know which one*), and it was necessary that they should not see me: I was hidden away in the second building which in principle was not part of the "Centre de Tri" and was only used for the accommodation of paras and for the mess.

I felt better and I managed to stand up and stay on my feet. I could sense from the different attitude of the paras

*It was in fact the Commission de Sauve-Garde represented by General Zeller.

F

toward me, that they regarded my refusal to speak as 'sporting'. Even the big para in Lo——'s group had changed his attitude. He came into my cell one morning and said to me:

'Were you tortured in the Resistance?'

'No; it's the first time,' I replied.

'You've done well,' he said with the air of a connoisseur. 'You're very tough.'

During the evening another para, whom I did not know, came in on his round. He was a short blond, with a strong northern accent, a conscript. He said to me with a big smile: 'You know, I was present all the time! My father talked to me about the Communists in the Resistance. They died, but they never talked. That's very fine!' I looked at this youth with his sympathetic face, who could talk of the sessions of torture I had undergone as if they were a football match that he remembered and could congratulate me without spite as he would a champion athlete. A few days later I saw him, shrivelled up and disfigured by hatred, hitting a Moslem who didn't go fast enough down the staircase. This "Centre de Tri" was not only a place of torture for Algerians, but a school of perversion for young Frenchmen.

One para at least was not like the others. He was young with a country accent. He opened the door of my cell towards seven o'clock at night, when there was nobody else in the corridor. He had a bag of provisions in his hand: cherries, chocolate, bread, some cigarettes. He offered them to me and said: 'Come on, take this. Excuse me, but here, one can't talk.' He shook my hand hard, very quickly, before closing the door. But Ir—— must have given orders, for I didn't see anyone else.

During the following days I was taken to the infirmary. The first time I went there my heart was beating. I feared a new injection of pentothal, but they only wanted to dress my infected wounds. I was given penicillin injections and several times my bandages were changed. I didn't know what to conclude from this attention. In any case it was in their interest to look after me: if they wanted to torture me again, I must not be too weak: if they decided on the other hand to execute me, they had to have (other than the normal bullet-wounds) a "clean" body in case of an autopsy. And with every day that passed my hopes grew that public opinion would be alerted and would succeed in rescuing me from their grasp, although at the same time I was convinced that they would rather face the scandal of my death than have me alive and able to reveal my experiences. They must have weighed that up themselves, because one of the paras said to me ironically, before I was able to stand by myself: 'It's a pity, isn't it? You could have told them enough to make a first-class row!'

They tried once again to question me. First Cha——, De—— and another whom I did not know. They made me come to the office on the same floor. I sat facing them and for the hundredth time they asked me the same questions, but more politely.

'Where did you spend the night before you were arrested?'

'I have already answered that question under torture,' I said to them. 'My answer is that I won't tell you.'

They smiled without insisting, then De—— said to me:

'The lease of your apartment—is it in your own name? You can answer that question: if you don't, the concierge will tell us. You can see for yourself it's not important.'

'Ask the concierge, if you like; I won't help you.'

The interview had not lasted more than two or three minutes and Cha—— accompanied me back to my cell.

A few days later I was visited by Lieutenant Ma——, the *aide de camp* of General M——. He started off by saying to me, without irony, that he was glad to see I was better. Then, very verbose, he gave me a "digest" of the political thought of the army of occupation in Algeria: 'We're not going to leave.' That was the theme. The miserable condition of the Algerians? One mustn't exaggerate. He knew a native who earned 80,000 francs a month. 'Colonialism?' A word invented by the defeatists. Yes, there had been injustices, but all that was finished now. Torture? You don't make war with choir-boys. The war would have been over a long time ago, but the Communists, the liberals and the sentimental press worked up opinion against the paras and hampered their "work". I had very little wish to get involved in a conversation of this nature: I only said to him that he was lucky that France had other representatives and other titles to glory; and otherwise, I thought it enough to answer his colonists' stereotyped arguments with a degree of irony.

Then he came to the object of his visit. They were making a new proposition to me: they were not going to ask me again to answer their questions, but only to write a brief of what I thought of the present political situation and the future of Algeria, after which I would be set free. Of course, I refused.

'Why?' he asked. 'Are you afraid that we will use it against you?'

'That, for one thing,' I answered. 'For another, I don't intend to help you. If you are interested in what my friends and I think of the Algerian problem, look at the old issues of the *Alger Républicain*: you have them all, as your paper, *Le Bled*, has taken over our offices.'

He did not press me further, and going to another subject he said to me point-blank: 'By the way, I had a visit from your wife and her lawyer. They asked me if you were alive. I answered that you were *still* alive.'

Then he went on: 'It's really a pity. I like you. And I admire your resistance. I'd like to shake your hand as I shall probably never see you again.' With this parting shot, he left.

On the evening of my departure for Lodi, one month after my arrest, I was taken into an office on one of the bottom floors. A captain of the paras, wearing the green beret of the Foreign Legion—was waiting for me: he wore a brush-cut, had a face like the blade of a knife which was slashed with long scars, thin wicked lips, and clear, prominent eyes. I sat down facing him and at the same moment he rose: with a single blow in the face, he threw me to the ground and knocked off my glasses, which had been returned to me: 'You're going to take that insolence off your face,' he said.

Lo—— had come in and was standing up near the window. The presence of this specialist made me think that more torture was about to follow. But the captain sat down again as I stood up.

'Do you want a cigarette?' he asked me, with a sudden change of tactics.

'No, I don't smoke, and I would prefer to be addressed as "vous".'

I didn't so much want to provoke him, as to know what he was leading up to: more torture or just a "friendly" talk? Whether or not he slapped me again, or just swallowed my remark, I felt that my fate was already decided. He replied that it was not important and from then on addressed me by the more formal "vous". I asked him if I could pick up my glasses: he thought my purpose was to remember his face better: 'You can look at me, if you want to. I am Captain Fau——, you know, the famous SS captain. You've heard the name before?' I was in the presence of Fau——— the head of the torturers at the Villa S———, whose reputation was particularly bloodthirsty.

He evidently regretted having let his hatred carry him away. He tried to talk calmly and, in order to wipe out the first impression, had two bottles of beer brought in. I drank slowly, looking at him out of the corner of my eye, in case another spasm of rage should cause him to throw the bottle in my teeth.

'You must have a nice dossier on me, haven't you? What would you do to me if the tables were turned?— but I think I know how to pick my risks.'

Then, in the same tone of voice, he embarked on a dissertation on Liberal or Communist writers, painters and intellectuals in general. He talked with a great deal of ignorance and with so much hatred that it changed the lines of his face, which was very mobile, into a skull-like grin. I let him go on talking, interrupting him sometimes with the sole purpose of gaining time and reducing that which would be devoted to torture, on the assumption that more torture was coming later.

He asked me the usual questions, but without insistence. Then he came back to politics. He walked around the room like a madman, coming up to me sometimes to shout a phrase in my face. He hoped that the war would spread to Tunisia and Morocco. He regretted that the Suez Expedition had not led to a general conflagration: 'I would have liked an American submarine to have attacked a French boat. We would have gone to war against the Americans: at least things would have been clear!' I contradicted him, but as one would contradict an invalid who must not be excited. Several times he wanted to hit me, but he restrained himself and once he shouted at me: 'You don't want to talk? As for me, I make them talk by putting a knife to their throats at night. I'll get you back one day.'

Without doubt, it was the intention of all of them to 'get me back', because they decided to send me to the camp at Lodi, which was reserved for suspects who could be removed at will.

But before this final questioning and the transfer which nothing had enabled me to foresee, I had been able during the month to observe how the torture factory worked. From my cell, I could see through the keyhole, part of the corridor, the landing and some of the stairs. The thin walls of the partition allowed me to hear the sounds of the neighbouring rooms.

During the day there was an incessant coming and going on the stairs and in the corridor: the paras, either alone, or pushing the imprisoned suspects brutally in front of them. On each floor—as I later found out—they kept fifteen or twenty persons in rooms which had been converted to dungeons. The prisoners slept on the cement itself or divided a mattress between three or four. They were constantly in darkness because the blinds were always closed so that nobody could see in from the houses opposite. During days, weeks, sometimes more than two months, they waited there either to be questioned, to be transferred to a camp or prison, or else to be the victim of an "attempt to escape", that is to say, a burst of machine-gun fire in the back.

Twice a day, at two o'clock and eight o'clock, when they didn't forget, we were given army biscuits—at five in the morning and five in the afternoon occasionally some bread and some spoonfuls of soup made from all the throw-outs of the meals of our overlords. One day I found a maggot, another time a paper label, and another time the stones spat out from some fruit.

It was a Moslem who was in charge of this distribution. Formerly a rifleman, he deserted to the maquis and was taken prisoner during the course of a battle. In exchange for his life, he had agreed to serve the paras. His name was Boula——, but for fun he had been put into a uniform which is called "Pour-la-France" and this is the name he was given. They had dressed him in a blue beret and armed him with a rubber truncheon, which he used on occasion in order to be more popular with his masters. This lackey was despised by everyone: by the paras as well as by the prisoners.

But it was at night that the "Centre de Tri" really came to life. I heard the preparations for expeditions: in the corridors there was a stamp of boots, of weapons, the orders of Ir——. Then, from the window, other noises came to me. In the court, jeeps and Dodges started up. Everything was silent for an hour or two, up to the time when they came back, their vehicles filled with "suspects" arrested during the course of the operation. I saw them, for an instant, as they passed through my field of vision:

the stairs, the landing and the corridors. Most often they were young men. They had hardly been given time to dress: some of them were still in pyjamas, others in bare feet or slippers. Sometimes there were also women. The latter were imprisoned in the right wing of the building.

The "Centre de Tri" was then filled with screams, insults, loud and brutal laughs. Ir—— would start to question an Arab. He shouted at him: 'Say your prayers to me.' And I could picture in the next room a man, humiliated to the roots of his soul, made to prostrate himself in an attitude of prayer before the lieutenant torturer. Then, all of a sudden, the first cries of the victim cut through the night. The real "work" of Ir——, of Lo—— and the others had begun.

One night, on the floor above me, they tortured a man: he was a Moslem, quite old, to judge by the sound of his voice. Between the terrible cries which the torture forced out of him, he said, exhausted: 'Vive la France! Vive la France!' Without doubt, he was hoping in this way to appease his tormentors. But the others continued to torture him and their laughs rang through the whole building.

When he didn't go on an operation, Ir—— and his men "worked" on the suspects who had previously been arrested. Towards midnight or one o'clock in the morning, a door of one of the prison rooms would open suddenly. The voice of a para would shout: 'Get up, you scum!' He called one, two, three names. Those who had been called out knew what awaited them. There was always a long silence and the para was always obliged to repeat the names a second time, which sent him into a fury: 'So you don't want to come then! Can't you say "here"?' Those who had been called out would get up and I could hear the blows which rained on them as the para pushed them before him.

One night, Ir—— sent out his men to assault all the rooms at once. Truncheon in hand, they hurled themselves into the cells. 'Get up!' The door of my cell, violently thrown open, slammed against the wall and I received a kick in the kidneys: 'Get up!' I got up, but Ir——, passing in the corridor, saw me and said: 'No, not him,' and slammed the door himself. I lay down again on my mattress, while a great rumpus of boots, blows and cries of pain invaded all the floors.

Every morning and evening, when Boula—— half opened the door to give me "my meal" or when I went to the privy, I would often pass Arab prisoners in the corridor, on the way back to their collective dungeon or cell. Some of them knew me from having seen me at political rallies organised by the paper: others only knew my name. I was always naked to the waist, still marked by the bruises I had received, my chest and hands covered with bandages. They understood that, like themselves, I had been tortured and they greeted me in the passage: 'Have courage, brother!' In their eyes I read a solidarity, a friendship, and such complete trust that I felt proud, particularly because I was a European, to be among them.

I lived like this for the space of a month, with the prospect of death always in front of me. It might happen that evening, it might be the next day at dawn. My sleep was still peopled with nightmares and nervous shocks which woke me with their violence. I was not surprised when one evening Cha—— came into my cell. It must have been about ten o'clock. I was standing up, near the window and looking towards the Boulevard Clemenceau where some few cars were still passing. He only said to me: 'Get ready; we're not going far.'

I put on my torn and dirty undershirt. In the corridor I heard him say: 'Get out Audin and Hadjadj; but we'll take them separately.' Ten times at least I had prepared myself for the last moments of this life which I thought I was about to leave. Once again, I thought of Gilberte, of all those I loved, of their atrocious pain. But I was exalted by the fight which I had survived without weakening, and by the thought that I would die as I had always hoped to die, true to my beliefs and to my companions in battle.

In the courtyard, I heard a car start, then move away. A moment later, in the direction of the Villa des Oliviers, I heard a long burst of machine-gun fire. I thought to myself: 'Audin.'

I stayed in front of the window for as long as possible to breathe the air of the night and to see the lights of the town. But minutes passed, hours passed and Cha—— did not come to get me.

My account is finished. Never have I written anything with so much difficulty. Perhaps it is because all these events are still fresh in my memory. Perhaps, too, it is because I have the idea that although this nightmare is behind me it is being lived by others as I am writing and that it ensures the continuation of this odious war. But I must tell everything I know. I owe it to Audin who "disappeared", and to all those who are being humiliated and tortured, and who still continue the struggle with courage. I owe it to all of them, who, each day, die for the liberty of their country.

I have written these lines four months after having left the paras, in cell 72 of the civil prison of Algiers.

It is only a few days since the blood of three young Algerians has joined that of the Algerian Fernand Yveton in the courtyard of the prison. In the immense cry of pain which sprang from the prisoners in all the cells at the moment when the executioner went to get the condemned, as in the absolute and solemn silence which followed it, the soul of Algeria vibrated. Its tears, shining in the darkness, fell across the bars of my cell. All the shutters had been closed by the guards, but we were able to hear one of the condemned cry out before he was gagged: 'Tahia El Djezair! Vive l'Algérie!' And with a single voice, at no doubt the very moment when the first of the three mounted the scaffold, the anthem of free Algeria rose from the women's section of the prison.

'Out of our struggle
Rise the voices of free men:
They claim independence
For our country.
I give you everything I love,
I give you my life,
O my country . . . O my country.'

All this, I have had to say for those Frenchmen who will read me. I want them to know that the Algerians do not confuse their torturers with the great people of France, from whom they have learnt so much and whose friendship is so dear to them.

But they must know what is done IN THEIR NAME.

November, 1957.

AFTERWORD

Henri Alleg

TRANSLATED BY DAVID L. SCHALK

Nearly fifty years have elapsed since the publication of this book, its subsequent seizure by the authorities, and its banning. The French government would not allow any challenge to the doctrines justifying the policy it was pursuing in Algeria.

If one were to listen to the men holding power, the struggle in Algeria had nothing to do with a people rising up against colonial oppression and determined to reclaim their independence. Such arguments were put forth, according to the authorities, only by the Communists and by a few wayward and naïve intellectuals. Algeria, our rulers had decreed, was an integral part of France, absolutely identical to Brittany or Alsace. In Algeria itself, only a handful of rebels, who would quickly be subdued by the "pacification" that was under way, were attempting to challenge this self-evident truth.

These, in summary, were the official arguments developed and the vocabulary used to hide the reality of military operations, which, for more than seven years, led to the massacre of hundreds of thousands of Algerians and the deaths of nearly thirty thousand French soldiers. But above all, what the authorities were attempting to hide were the methods employed to bring an entire people to its knees: the destruction of hundreds of villages by bombs and napalm, the imprisonment of thousands of suspects, the torturing of captured political activists and military combatants, and well beyond that, the torture of all the protesters and witnesses the government could get its hands on—massacres, rapes, and summary executions disguised as "attempted escapes" or "disappearances."

Such was the sinister balance sheet that contradicted the proclamations of the civil and military leaders. They pretended to engage in a just and "clean" war, portraying themselves as respectful of universal moral values and of human rights, which France had so often, verbally at least, championed.

It was precisely this presentation of reality that *The Question*—in French, the word signifies "torture"—demonstrated to be false. This is why this book, whose pages were spirited out almost one by one from the prison in Algiers where I was incarcerated, was judged scandalous by the partisans of a war to the finish, was denounced as a "tissue of lies," and ultimately banned. On the other hand, it aroused the interest of millions of French men and women who refused to let themselves be deceived and who demanded that the truth be told. Reprinted or recopied secretly, sometimes in a truly makeshift fashion, in tens of thousands of copies, it was quickly known in all of France, despite the decree that prohibited its distribution.

Once Algerian independence was acquired in July 1962, those who had fought tooth and nail against that outcome, waging an unjust and "imbecilic" war (the word is a prime minister's), stubbornly insisted on denying the evidence. Carefully calibrated amnesty laws, passed during the presidencies of Charles de Gaulle and François Mitterrand, were able to whitewash the activities of the torturers and protect them from any potential legal action.

These very torturers, secure under the umbrella of amnesty, did not hesitate to file defamation lawsuits against journalists and witnesses who dared to remind the public of their sanguinary and barbarous exploits. The best known of these vile and vicious individuals were feted as heroes, promoted in rank, and decorated with the highest military and civilian honors.

Through silence, disinformation when the silence was broken, open censorship (as in the case of the banning of films dealing with the Algerian conflict), or a discreet and camouflaged censorship, our leaders endeavored to cultivate a generalized ignorance, a complete forgetting of what had happened. Ten or fifteen years after the return of peace, lycée graduates had hardly heard anything about the war itself, and even less about the terrible brutalities that accompanied it. Such knowledge was simply deleted from school curricula.

Not until October 1999, forty-five years after the first shots were fired in the Aurès Mountains, did the French government finally acknowledge that a "war" had taken place in Algeria. Prior to that admission, a conflagration that had caused immeasurable death and destruction was officially categorized as merely "police operations."

Then, in November 2000, under the pressure of public opinion and following the extraordinarily gripping account by an Algerian woman of the arrest, torture, and rape she had suffered at the hands of French soldiers forty-three years earlier, further "progress" was made. President Jacques Chirac and his prime minister, Lionel Jospin, were obliged to admit that torture and assassination had indeed been endemic during this period. Indirectly they went as far as acknowledging that those who had dared to denounce the torturers and their powerful allies, and who had in turn been insulted, libeled, and sued for damages, had indeed told the truth. In fact, the liars were those political and military leaders who had ordered these criminal acts, covered them up, and ultimately denied that they had happened. But neither Jacques Chirac nor Lionel Jospin went as far as to solemnly condemn, in the name of France, these ignoble activities, as was being asked of them by numerous organizations and personalities.

Paradoxically, it was two generals, Jacques Massu and Paul

Aussaresses, who, much against their will, finally also contributed to the recovery of the truth. General Massu, the former commander in chief of the forces of repression in the Algerian capital, conceded shortly before his death that torture had systematically been carried out by the soldiers under his command, particularly during the "Battle of Algiers." He now belatedly regretted these practices, for "we could have proceeded without them."

In a shameful book, Paul Aussaresses, who held the rank of major at the time, had the audacity to take credit for, and actually revel in, his crimes. He ordered the summary executions of dozens of Algerians who had been arrested in random sweeps. He also bragged about numerous "exemplary actions," including having put to death with his own hands two Algerian prisoners, principal leaders of the National Liberation Front (FLN). Then he disguised these crimes as suicides. Confronted with the public outcry generated by these cynical confessions, General Aussaresses was obliged to appear before a tribunal, which ordered him to pay a substantial fine. Thus he was punished, but not for the crimes he had committed. The amnesty laws passed decades earlier protected him from any criminal liability. Rather, the fine was levied because he bragged publicly of having perpetrated these crimes.

Additionally, following an official request issued by the French president, Aussaresses's name was stricken from the rolls of the Legion of Honor. When one considers the monstrosity of the crimes committed, these were absolutely minimal sanctions.

Nevertheless, the very fact that these punishments, however benign, were meted out is indicative of a shift in views among the French judicial and political elites. For the first time, an officer who had both ordered and carried out torture himself had been brought to justice and received a legal condemnation.

These and related developments help us to comprehend why, even fifty years after its outbreak, the Algerian war remains a subject of passionate interest for millions of French adults. They are encouraging the young among them to read *The Question*, in order to comprehend the true history of their nation, even its darkest moments, and to alert the rising generation to be on the lookout for any possible return to barbarism.

But there is yet another explanation, even more contemporary, for the renewal of interest in issues raised by *The Question*. This explanation moves beyond the boundaries of France. We know that French specialists in "muscular interrogation," or "extreme questioning" (the habitual euphemisms for torture), were able to pursue new careers well beyond the borders of Algeria as soon as the conflict ended there in July 1962. With the authorization of their superiors in the cabinet ministries and the military general staff, General Aussaresses and his fellow officers responded positively to the solicitations of Latin American dictators. These rulers, many of them former military men, had need of the particular talents of their French colleagues to enable them to suppress their populations, which were becoming more and more resistant to their tyrannical rule.

During the years of apartheid, the rulers of South Africa also called upon these professionals for their help and advice. In various countries, including the United States, numerous intelligence officers thus received training in the tasks they would be asked to perform. They were initiated into the methods of the "French school," with their instructors being former torturers during the Algerian War. This "instructional model," which we have recently seen in operation in Iraq, at the Abu Ghraib prison and elsewhere, and at Guantanamo Bay in Cuba, is still widely emulated. We have every reason to believe that it will continue to be practiced well into the future.

For a long time it has been a characteristic of governing elites to devote themselves to the interests of the powerful, rather than to the welfare of the masses. Fraudulently they continue to invoke the "barbarian menace" of terrorism. They respond to the grave problems that assail our world—social injustice, frustration, misery, inequality, sickness, and hunger—by a refusal to listen, to understand. Instead they give us war, violence, and torture.

And this is why it is always useful for those who retain a belief in peace, and a hope for a better future, not to forget the lessons of the past, even when they are painful to contemplate.